THE HAPPY VALLEY

1. Family group in "Uplawn" living room: standing (l. to r.) Paul Dakin, George Dakin; seated (top row) Anna Maria Olcott Dakin, Jessie Messmore Dakin; seated (bottom row) Leonard Dakin, Florence Dakin

THE HAPPY VALLEY

The Elegant Eighties in Upstate New York

PAULINE DAKIN TAFT

photographs by Leonard Dakin

foreword by Louis C. Jones
appendix by Beaumont Newhall

SYRACUSE UNIVERSITY PRESS

IN LOVING MEMORY OF MY FATHER, LEONARD DAKIN,
WHO NEVER KNEW THAT HIS WORK WOULD LIVE

Foreword

MORE THAN FIFTEEN YEARS AGO we invited Pauline Dakin Taft
to the New York State Historical Association in Cooperstown to give
a lecture in which she showed the photographs taken by her father,
Leonard Dakin, in the 1880's and told stories about her father and
the people who appeared in the pictures. This was long before *Life*
or *American Heritage* or any of the other publications that later
discovered Dakin's work had made the photographs famous, but
that evening had a very interesting effect on me. Cherry Valley is a
neighboring village to our own and in the course of events one travels
through it many times in a year, but never again did I go through it
without remembering some aspect of life which had been recorded
by Leonard Dakin or his daughter. Somehow the later Victorian
period was given a new warmth, a new quality of life and laughter.
Now Mrs. Taft has expanded her earlier lectures into permanent
form, and this is what lies ahead of you. I know of no other volume
that combines so successfully a body of family lore and family photographs to create a document of significant social history.

Over the years we have become very much interested in the Dakin family and its ancillary branches: the Mumfords, the Olcotts, the
Campbells, the Perrys, and many others. Our library at Cooperstown
has long owned the Mumford papers, going back into the business
transactions of the family in the eighteenth century. In 1963 we
acquired a bushel basketful of the correspondence of Samuel Dana
Dakin, the grandfather of Leonard Dakin. This was a man who

graduated from college, like his father and sons, who tutored for a while, then became part-owner of a newspaper and literary journal, who wrote poetry and traveled with the Knickerbocker set, a lawyer who invented a drydock, a man whose education continued all through his life and who was in every sense a successful person.

Indeed, this family is a very appropriate one to study, because they were, like many other similar families in small towns, the Establishment. These were people of integrity, industry, and intelligence. They were the lawyers and bankers and businessmen. It is time to reassess families of this quality who suffered from the literary men of the 1930's. We are now far enough away from both their time and the time of their original detractors so that we can take a fresh look and see what these well-endowed people were really like. This book gives us a sense of how they saw themselves.

Certain members of the Dakin family lived in Cherry Valley year in and year out, but the majority of the branches lived elsewhere and came back each summer for their vacations. Several branches still return to Cherry Valley in July and August. There are in upstate New York a whole group of handsome villages where some of the oldest families are the summer families; there was a time when their ancestors lived and worked there the year 'round, but that was six or seven generations ago. The call of the place continues and will not be silenced.

The hasty reader of this volume may get the impression that it is a book of pictures pasted together with a little text. This is to misunderstand the book and its virtues. Primarily this is a book about a family, its members, its houses, its summer way of life, its "sense of well-being and security." The text is a remarkable collection of family lore, well told, and neatly intertwined with Dakin's unusual collection of amateur photographs. The text and photographs are mutually supportive and interdependent. The text, like the photographs, gives us insight into a total way of life, into a segment of society now long gone and little understood.

The mood is established by the fact that always it is summer-time, vacation time, there are few words and no pictures of work, of jobs, of school; it is summer in the country for city families, city families composed of closely linked brothers and sisters and cousins and friends of cousins. One is aware of a great deal of laughter and gaiety. There is time each day for tennis and croquet or archery; in the evening there are parlor games and parlor drama. For the older members of the clan there is music and poetry, Shakespeare and Dickens read aloud and scenes from Gilbert and Sullivan sung and enjoyed. These are healthy, active, intelligent teenagers with their parents and grandparents, with their friends and younger kinsfolk.

Mrs. Taft has whittled away at many of the cliches about the last quarter of the nineteenth century; there are stories of children in church, but it is in a church that is unoppressive, one in which the Devil is not waiting in the corner to grab the wayward child; hers was a family that could remember one of their youngsters stealing and eating the communion bread and his logical, if untheological, explanation, "But I was hungry." It was a family where one of the boys could get involved in a court case with a nearby rapscallion over a fighting cock and the family could enjoy it without a sense of loss of face. There is much about courtship, but this was courtship unencumbered by the traditional chaperon and her prying. There is much about marriage and what Mrs. Taft refers to as the "qualities of connubial restraint," yet she also makes it perfectly clear that beneath the formalities of married life there was great love and affection, a warmth that began with the older couples and permeated the entire group. We see the naive innocence we traditionally think of as part of the Victorian maiden's mental equipment, but we see it in sharp contrast to a sister who is thinking in terms of women's rights and women's education. All of this material adds to our understanding of the structure of the family, its internal relationships, its pressures and releases.

The interest of the reader curious about social history will find passages and pictures of unending interest. Much is said and much is shown of men's and women's styles, of dress materials, dressmaking, the sources of patterns, and the sources of styles; there is even interesting information about Victorian falsies. Mrs. Taft has pointed out the change in the style of men's beards and has some fresh comments on men's sports clothes, the traditions, taboos, and niceties of smoking, and the changes that took place in those taboos. There is much in this book about household decor—both in the text and in the pictures—but much, too, about plumbing, bathtubs, indoor and outdoor toilets. This was a family that was very fond of its gardens, and one is deeply impressed by their luxuriousness. In an age when we see departments of public works ruthlessly cutting down all the handsome trees along village streets, one looks with envy and self-pity at photographs of the rich, shaded thoroughfares winding through villages, for we live in a time that no longer understands the virtue of the tree.

The book gives us valuable information about roadways, toll gates, the mud that slowed down travel, the variety of horse-drawn vehicles, the construction of bridges, the style of street lamps. I could go on piling up a long list of the detail that is available in this volume, but one wants to leave some of the fun to the reader.

This, then, is life as summer people knew it, summer people with deep roots in a community they loved and returned to each year; here is a complex of several large, related families whose parents and grandparents had known each other, grown up together, played and sorrowed side by side over many decades. True, it is one segment of a society in one small village in one season of the year, but what is seen is seen sharply in great detail and reflects much more than it says.

Leonard Dakin was an ingenious and creative photographer with a sure sense of selection and a capacity for focusing sharply on his subject. By the same token, his daughter selects her anecdotes for their telling effects, their appropriateness, and the way in which each story reflects a whole pattern of life. Pauline Dakin Taft's prose and Leonard Dakin's photography are mutually supportive and produce a happy book about a happy valley.

LOUIS C. JONES

Cooperstown, New York
Spring, 1965

Preface

TWENTIETH-CENTURY AMERICA developed from the small town. This book—neither history nor fiction—tries to convey the flavor of small-town American life in the late nineteenth century through contemporary photographs taken by Leonard Dakin in Cherry Valley, New York.

As the photographer's daughter, I have been able to amplify and explain this photographic record with old family tales. Although memory may become somewhat inaccurate with time, such family recollections as these do preserve the spirit of an era. Together with the photographs they present a vivid document of one aspect of life during an important decade in America, the 1880's.

Arnold J. Toynbee wrote in *Civilization on Trial* (Oxford University Press, 1948) that the middle-class English at the turn of the century regarded history, for them, as over. It came to an end in foreign affairs in 1815, with the Battle of Waterloo; in home affairs in 1832, with the great Reform Bill; and in imperial affairs in 1859, with the suppression of the Indian Mutiny. And this belief in the permanent state of felicity which this ending of history had conferred on them was shared by the middle-class people of the United States in the North, for whom history had come to an end with the winning of the West and the federal victory in the Civil War. For these middle-class people, he says, God's work of creation was completed, and "behold it was very good."

In this book I attempt to depict the unalloyed contentment and complacency of that bygone age when there were no cold wars or atomic secrets. To make this picture come alive I tell the story of one family in a small country town, a family of no particular distinction, whose history is typical of similar families throughout the country. But this family was fortunate in having a son who preserved in photographs so rare a record of the spirit of genteel living in the eighties as to be considered a unique contribution to Americana.

Leonard Dakin was not thinking of posterity when he took these pictures; nor were the young people in them. These girls and boys were enjoying the pastimes of a happy summer's day, not looking beyond the present. We are fortunate that my father became interested in a new fad—the camera. Running a large orange grove in Florida during the winter and spending the summer with his parents in the North gave him time for his latest hobby. To be sure, he recorded only one side of life in this period. Jacob Riis has shown the other side in his photographic indictment of New York slums during the eighties and nineties, *How the Other Half Lives*. *The Happy Valley* is a story of American life in its "more smiling aspects," as William Dean Howells put it.

These pictures put blood, life, and laughter back into the eighties, at a time when action shots were not yet commonplace and head clamps were still in general use. They belie the somber faces and the grim figures usually seen in the old family album on the parlor table. Few amateurs in those days were artists at heart as my father was. Edward Steichen has said, "Only a photographer that was an artist could evoke the grace and charm of a place and a period as Leonard Dakin has done."

Sometime in the nineties he carefully laid away his glass-plate negatives—each one in a manila envelope properly numbered and labeled. It was sixty years later that his youngest son, Herbert, found some two hundred of them in the barn of the old family homestead. As we were clearing away the debris of years when the home was broken up, there, behind curve-topped trunks filled with hooped skirts and finely pleated bosom shirts, Herbert found the negatives in a great wooden box. Time and the rats had taken their toll, some of the plates were cracked and stained, but most of them were amazingly well preserved. All credit is due the son who in time of stress recognized their value at once and rescued them from oblivion.

The photographs in this book range in years from 1865 to 1899, but most of them were taken in the latter half of the 1880's. All those definitely not taken by my father are marked with a credit line. Of the others my father took all but a few, which cannot be determined with certainty. For the stills in which he appears, he used an improvised timing mechanism. For the action pictures with him in them, he probably set up his camera and asked his brother Paul or a friend to snap the picture.

I could never have attempted this book without the tender interest and wise counsel of my beloved husband, Arthur Irving Taft. Its many shortcomings may be attributed to the fact that I lost him when the work was barely started.

I was given inestimable help by my patient and long-suffering relatives who were young people in these pictures and whom I bombarded with questions about the 1880's. I am especially grateful for such aid to my uncle, Paul Worth Dakin, my aunt, Florence Dakin, and my cousins, Marion Olcott Dix, Lucy Olcott Perry, Harriet Olcott Campbell, J. Perry Olcott, Mary Campbell Gardiner, Anna Miles Olcott, Ellie Dakin Chamberlain, Harriet Campbell Green, Alice L. Fowler, and Sophie Foster Sofio. Through them and the generous help of Rosamond Swinnerton Lum, Major Abraham Beekman Cox, Cornelia Schwartz, Mary White Woltge, and Levere Winne, I have verified old stories and learned new ones. It is largely their first-hand testimony that gives authority to these pages.

For encouragement, information, advice, and other kindnesses, I wish to thank the following persons: my cousins, Douglas Worth Olcott, Julia Campbell Bates, Olcott Worth Dakin, and Arthur H. Bond; also, Virgil Barker, Andrew C. Ritchie, Louis C. Jones, Beaumont Newhall, George W. Rosner, Mary Irwin, Blanche Sawyer Duncan, Marjory Stoneman Douglas, and Carl Snyder. I wish to thank Edward Steichen and Arnold J. Toynbee for permission to quote them in this book.

To my sorrow, many of the above have passed away without seeing the result of their kindness.

I wish to pay special tribute here to the late Hazel Barker King, for many years curator of the Dudley Peter Allen Memorial Art Museum in Oberlin, Ohio, who first saw prints of these photographs at my home. She recognized immediately not only their historical and sociological value but, with the greatest of enthusiasm, their artistic value as well. She arranged at once for an exhibition of one hundred of the enlarged photographs in the Oberlin Museum.

Since then they have been shown in many art museums and historical societies throughout the country, where Leonard Dakin has been acclaimed as an artist who, as Edward Steichen has commented, "richly merits the recognition his work is now receiving."

PAULINE DAKIN TAFT

Coconut Grove, Florida
Spring, 1965

Contents

Illustrations

PART ONE

Cherry Valley, 1830-1880

Grandparents

IN 1830 HORATIO JOSIAH OLCOTT, the ninth of Josiah and Deborah Olcott's thirteen children, set out from Hudson, New York, to seek his fortune. Wishing to be a banker, he decided to start his career in the thriving little town of Cherry Valley, some fifty-two miles west of Albany. After visiting a brother who was a banker in Albany, he climbed aboard a four-horse stagecoach and joined the endless string of passenger coaches, emigrant wagons, and broad-wheeled freight wagons bumping slowly over the Great Western Turnpike.

Since Horatio had never before been farther from home than Albany, he was interested in everything he saw, from the ornate coach and the broadside stating that the fare was calculated according to one's weight, to the long, wide leather supports that reduced the violence of the jolts. It did not take long for Horatio to see why one of the coach companies was called ''The Shake Gut Line.''

The Great Western Turnpike had been started thirty years earlier, when a charter was granted for a coach road from Albany to John Walton's Tavern in Cherry Valley. Three years later it was extended farther west and the stockholders of the company were allowed to pay for their subscriptions in labor. The road followed the old Seneca Indian Trail, winding up and down hills among the stumps of ancient oaks and beeches, through forests and clearings, past log cabins and frame farmhouses, over bumpy log causeways, and through rushing fords.

Pull-out places were occasionally provided for passing, which must have been precarious at best but hazardous when the coach overtook a huge Conestoga freight wagon, with its six to ten great horses, or long droves of cattle, horses, mules, hogs, and sheep being driven westward on the hoof. These Conestoga wagons did not have to pay toll when they rumbled through a toll gate every four or five miles because the iron rims of their ponderous wheels were six to ten inches wide and helped flatten the ruts in the road. The driver, astride a wheel horse, would remove his foot-long stogy to shout a greeting to the stagecoach as it swept by him at five-and-a-half miles an hour.

Instead of gas stations along the way, there were little taverns—sixty-two in the fifty-two miles between Albany and Cherry Valley alone and fifteen more in the village of Cherry Valley. Horatio was glad to stretch his legs at the end of the first twelve miles when they stopped at one of these taverns for a new relay of horses. Here wagers were running high as drivers pitched quoits or engaged in wrestling matches. One, a man named Slocum, who lived in Cherry Valley, claimed to be the champion wrestler of the state. At any of these taverns Horatio had a good meal for sixpence and paid another sixpence for a night's lodging.

As his coach began to climb to the northernmost terrace of the Catskill highland, Horatio left his place inside and clambered up to the seat beside the driver. From him he learned much of the Indian

2. Cherry Valley from Willow Hill, looking toward "Uplawn"

lore and history of the country through which they passed. When the driver heard that Horatio intended to settle in Cherry Valley, he applauded his choice, saying that it was a town of distinction, a great crossroads, indeed one of the leading towns in the center of New York State.

Almost a hundred years before this four leading men of Albany had obtained a patent of eight thousand acres in this beautiful valley, known then only to the Indians. One of them, an enterprising Scotchman, John Lindesay, had brought his little family and built an isolated home, sixteen miles from the nearest settlement on the Mohawk River, with only an ancient Indian trail connecting them. This was a favorite hunting ground of the Mohawks, whose friendship Lindesay cultivated. Only the succor of a friendly Indian narrowly saved the Lindesays from starvation that first bitter winter. On snowshoes he brought them a bag of provisions on his back all the way from the river.

This experience led Lindesay to enlist the efforts of his friend, the Rev. Samuel Dunlop, who in 1741 brought six Scotch-Irish families from New Hampshire with him to found the village of Cherry Valley. They made the voyage around Cape Cod and up the Hudson by sloop, slowly tacking for two weeks. The merchants of Albany furnished them fresh supplies and tools, and they pushed westward along the Mohawk in batteaux. The last sixteen miles to Cherry Valley they covered on foot, following the old Seneca Trail. Soon after they had built their rude log cabins, they established there the first English-speaking church and the first classical school west of

3. In 1830 Horatio Olcott traveled over the Great Western Turnpike by stage-coach from Albany to Cherry Valley

was indiscriminate; terror reigned. Those who had not escaped or been held for ransom were brutally killed and scalped, and all their homes and barns were burned to the ground. But immediately upon the close of the war the survivors returned to Cherry Valley to build new homes on the ashes of the old and to recultivate the soil now overgrown with wild cherry and sumac.

Horatio listened intently to the driver's tales of the past, and it was only with real effort that he came back to the present. He was eager to meet the descendants of those brave survivors and to hear more of the story from them. The driver told him that after the peace the great westward exodus had begun, and since Cherry Valley was on the main route of travel from New England and eastern New York to the new territories of the West, it soon became the most important settlement south of the Mohawk and west of Albany.

Horatio's father had favored his son's choice of Cherry Valley, for through business acquaintances there he knew that although its population never exceeded a thousand the town was the home of a greater number of men of ability and prominence than any other place in the center of New York. For example, Dr. Joseph White, who was the first president of the Cherry Valley Bank, a state senator, and the first county judge, lived here. A distinguished surgeon and president of the New York State Medical Association, he always had six or eight graduate medical students working with him. Together they covered New York on horseback from Albany to Buffalo. Cherry Valley provided congressmen, senators, lawyers, and judges as political leaders. Men high in military circles lived there, too. More-

5. September 6, 1888. Cherry Valley from Lancaster Hill. Old Civil War barracks at left

over, the village boasted the first bank west of the Hudson River. No wonder young Horatio Olcott was happy to start his banking career there!

When the stagecoach reached Prospect Hill House, a famous old tavern only three miles east of Cherry Valley, all the passengers got out to marvel at the magnificent panorama northward across the Mohawk Valley to the Adirondacks. At last they rounded the final bend and reached the height that marked the watershed between the Mohawk and Susquehanna Valleys. From here they had their first glimpse of Cherry Valley. The little town seemed deeply buried in the green of elms and maples, with only roofs and church steeples projecting, a pretty little village nestled in hills.

With sounding horn the coach clattered down the hill at the foot of which stood Elisha Flint's Tavern, a favorite overnight stop for men heading west with droves of cattle and turkeys. Its red brick walls were eighteen inches thick. (Horatio's grandson was to buy it a hundred years later for a summer home.) The driver cracked his whip as they proceeded down Main Street and tooted his horn as they drew up with a flourish before the oldest tavern in this section of the country, Tryon House. Here the noise and bustle of stable boys shouting as they changed horses, the cheering of spectators at the inevitable quoits game, and the laughter and greetings of new arrivals and their friends excited Horatio's wonder—so much activity in such a small village so far from any big cities!

But he learned that in addition to the great through turnpike connecting New England and Albany with Buffalo and the West and

6. View of the Mohawk Valley from Prospect Hill House, three miles east of
Cherry Valley

the one connecting the Mohawk River with the Susquehanna Valley, there were nine local coach lines operating in this small crossroads town. Then he could understand why it was so difficult to find black-smiths enough to keep Cherry Valley's hundred and ten stage horses in shoes when the stream of travel was at its height. The rapid growth of the country to the west and this enormous traffic passing through the village made Cherry Valley the important and pros-perous trading center it was.

Horatio found plenty of cash or barter stores handling unusual merchandise, as many as ten retail liquor stores, a brewery, many enterprising industries such as tanneries, last factories, truss works, a brass foundry, a marble works, and a cabinet shop, as well as artisans of exceptional skill. There were the white-bearded clock maker, Edward Prescott, whose clocks, made entirely by hand and largely of wood, are still highly prized, and the noted silversmith, Harry Smith, a jeweler whose exhibit at the Crystal Palace in 1851 was considered the finest piece of workmanship shown. Amasa Belknap was a well-known gunsmith who filled large orders for rifles from as far away as Texas. Most of the virgin soil of New York and Ohio was overturned by the cast-iron plows made in Cherry Valley, and most of the farms in the countryside boasted a melodeon, or "parlor organ," which was invented and manufactured there. Such was the thriving town where Horatio Olcott found himself as he clutched his carpetbag and set out in search of lodgings.

We have two photographs of Main Street, by which Horatio entered the village. The kerosene-lamp post seen in Plate 8 was not

7. The "Happy Valley," where Horatio chose to start his career as cashier in the bank

there in 1830. It was some twenty-five years before Horatio would see the young lamplighter taking his girl with him on his rounds to light these street lamps, a short ladder slung over one shoulder and his cleaning materials and can of oil over the other. This corner (where the village library now stands) was called "Old Maid Smiths' Corner," named for the three Smith sisters who lived there.

The photograph of Monument Square (Plate 11) shows a portion of the National Central Bank of Cherry Valley which was founded in 1818, only twelve years before Horatio arrived to take his place in the village as cashier of this bank. Here he found not only his life work but the man who was to become his life-long friend, David Little.

Horatio soon learned that David was engaged to the pretty sixteen-year-old Julia Seelye. At the Seelye house David introduced Horatio to his fiancée, who liked him immediately. That very evening she wrote a letter to her dearest friend, Harriet Leonard, in Suffield, Connecticut (Julia's family had only recently come to Cherry Valley from Suffield), and invited Harriet to visit her. "For now there is another young man in the bank," she wrote, "named Horatio Olcott. And my father is going to Suffield soon on business and could bring you back with him." Julia folded the letter carefully, sealed it with wax, addressed it on the back, and posted it. Then she waited with pleasant anticipation for the reply.

Harriet was a charming, ingenuous girl of sixteen. Her father, Capt. Daniel Leonard, had been lost at sea in the War of 1812, six months before Harriet was born. Her mother, Sarah, had returned to

8. Cherry Valley's Main Street (at Maid Smiths' Corner), by which Horatio
entered the village

Suffield to live in the crowded household of her parents, the Aldens. There her baby Harriet grew up with Sarah's eleven younger brothers and sisters. As preparations for Harriet's visit to Cherry Valley were made, all the family were excited about what might happen there. Since she had no gown equal to the occasion, they decided that she should wear the best black silk of the aunt nearest her size.

When Mr. Seelye arrived Harriet was ready and eager to start. The two set out by stagecoach from Suffield, traveling in one of the new flat-topped Concord coaches with six horses. They journeyed to Cherry Valley by way of New York, where Mr. Seelye bought two coal-scuttle bonnets of blue satin—both allegedly for his daughter Julia. Next day they set out with the bonnets in immense bandboxes tied on top of the stagecoach. When they arrived home Mr. Seelye gave one of the bonnets to Harriet, who was thoroughly surprised and delighted. She remembered for many years the sensation she and Julia caused when they appeared in their new hats at church that Sunday.

When Julia introduced her friend to David, Harriet told him playfully that now she must captivate the young cashier, Horatio Olcott. But no sooner had she decided upon this course than the young law student, Oliver Morse (cousin of Samuel F. B. Morse, the inventor), began to pay her court. She was drawn at once to Oliver and admired him deeply, even letting him hold her hand once on a picnic. For this she felt so guilty afterwards that she spent hours on her knees asking forgiveness. But in spite of Oliver's attractions, Harriet soon confided to Julia that she could hardly resist Horatio's

9. Main Street (looking northeast) as seen from the bank

greater intelligence. He had already absorbed the Indian lore of the country and could hold her spellbound with his tales. Horatio and Harriet were married the very next summer, when she was seventeen and he was twenty-one. (Their daughter Grace later married the son of Oliver Morse.)

It was no doubt the influence of her grandparents, who thought Harriet should marry the rising young banker rather than the student, that made Harriet choose Horatio. For, many years later, she told her favorite granddaughter that she did not love her husband when she married him. It was not until they were settled in their own home and he used to pull her down on his knee and sing his lovely Scottish ballads that she fell in love with him. When a grandchild asked her if she was ever sorry she had married him, she replied, "Sorry? My dear, it was the best thing I ever did in my life!"

In this period of great financial prosperity for Cherry Valley, at least a dozen of its citizens were worth more than $50,000—a great fortune in those days—and several others were worth well over $100,000; but the panic of 1837 reduced many of these fortunes. Horatio, however, had little to start out with and never became wealthy.

He built his young bride a large square house on a deep lot between the Academy and the Presbyterian Church. They named it "Woodbine," because of the lush growth of that vine over the porches and garden trellises. As time passed and the family grew, the Olcotts added rooms here and there, built extensions on different levels making many steps up and down from one room to another, added a

10. Soldiers' Monument erected to commemorate the forty-two Civil War victims from Cherry Valley

third story over the original part, and put porches on every side. The end result was a delightful, rambling, roomy house, comfortable to the core and loved by the children and grandchildren to the last timber and clapboard.

Horatio and Harriet's first child was a little girl whom they named for their dear friend Julia, who had introduced them. Three years later Anna Maria was born. It was she who would become the mother of our photographer, Leonard Dakin. Within the next four years the Olcotts had two little boys, Egbert and Horatio Leonard. Then Harriet, a mature matron of twenty-six, began to wear a cap. She and her mother, who lived with them, both had a great variety of caps, plain- or lace-ruffled, with black, white, or mauve ribbons to suit every occasion. The younger boy, Horatio, was eight years old when another little brother arrived, Arthur Leonard, whom they called Lenny. The only shadow in the happy life of this family was the death of little Lenny at the age of nine.

It was sixteen years after this that their last child was born, a little girl named Grace Vernon. She was her father's special pet and was less restrained than the other children. There is a family story of how Gracie, at the age of six, was wakened one night when her father was sitting up later than usual, reading by candlelight. Her mother went to the stairs and called down, "Mr. Olcott, do come to bed." The next morning at breakfast Gracie remarked, "Mother, if you don't know Father well enough to call him by his name, I don't think you know him well enough to call him to come to bed with you."

It was this same little Gracie who at the age of four embarrassed

11. Alden Street and Monument Square (looking south)

her shy sister, Anna Maria, when she was engaged to George Dakin. George was fond of the child, and in a letter of sympathy to Annie, who was seriously ill, he had said, "Kiss my sweet Gracie on her soft neck for me." When Annie was convalescing and George was able to get to Cherry Valley to visit her, it was little Gracie who happened to meet him at the door. In response to his anxious inquiry about Annie's condition, little Gracie told him (just as Annie herself appeared) that she was quite well again now "because for a whole week she has been able to come downstairs to go out back!" Annie fled to her room and refused to see her lover until she had regained her composure.

Annie's fiancé, George Dakin, lived in Utica, but he and his four brothers came frequently to Cherry Valley and Cooperstown for parties and dances with the young people, among whom they had many friends. Indeed, Annie's and George's parents had long known each other and the ladies even exchanged favorite recipes, the kind that said, "Add six more eggs and beat an hour longer."

George's grandfather, Samuel Dakin, had brought his family from Jaffrey, New Hampshire, to Utica, New York, about the time Annie's grandfather settled in Hudson. Samuel practiced law in Utica with an old Dartmouth College friend.

George's father, Samuel Dana Dakin, the eldest of seven children, graduated from Hamilton College in 1821, then studied law in Utica. He was only twenty-three when he became the owner and editor of the Utica *Sentinel and Gazette* and began to publish poetry. A letter to his college friend, Elihu Mumford, in 1824 reflects his

12. The Isaac Seelye House on Alden Street, where Horatio met his fiancée, Harriet Leonard

literary interests. In speaking of the Lyceum he wrote, "We were favored with the presence of all the beauty, fashion and intelligence of Utica, and the discussion was lively and interesting on the subject, 'Have Works of the Imagination a Beneficial Tendency?' We really begin to entertain some hopes that a literary spirit may at length be roused from its present dormant state."

When Samuel met his friend's sixteen-year-old sister, he wrote Elihu, "Why didn't you tell me you had such a beautiful sister? She is the most fascinating woman I have ever met." The Mumford family, who lived in Cayuga, New York, and had extensive land speculations in the western part of the state, often exchanged visits with the Dakins in Utica. They sent their "fascinating" daughter, Mary Pierce Mumford, to the Ladies' Seminary in Troy. There, shortly after New Year's Day in 1826, she received a jubilant letter from Samuel saying that her father had consented to their "attachment and union. How sweet, my love, is this gratification!" Then he added, "Tomorrow I make calls to pay the compliments of the season and get all the New Year's kisses that I can.* Would that you were in the sphere of my calls; I should be sure then of one kiss sweeter than all the rest put together." They were married in September, 1827, and lived in Utica.

Samuel was a versatile man: he practiced law, was successful in business, and invented improvements in the design of drydocks and marine railways. These he patented and with his associate, Ruther-

---

*Collecting kisses from the ladies on New Year's calls was a general custom of the times.

13. The Olcott homestead, "Woodbine," which Horatio built for his bride in 1831

ford Moody, he constructed floating drydocks for the United States Navy Department at Philadelphia and other naval shipyards.

Samuel and Mary Dakin had five sons and two daughters; George was the third son. In 1839 they moved their family to New York City, where Samuel practiced law and contributed prose and poetry to the *Knickerbocker Monthly*. Later they moved to Dobbs Ferry on the Hudson River, where he was preparing a history of civil liberties and planning to build a country estate three miles from "Sunnyside," the home of his friend Washington Irving, when these dreams ended in his sudden death from a heart attack.

At this time their four older sons were at Hamilton College. George graduated in 1853 and received his M.A. there in 1856, one year before he married Annie Olcott in Cherry Valley.

14. Samuel and Mary Dakin's five sons in 1839: (l. to r.) Francis E. Dakin,
Henry Mumford Dakin, George William Bethune Dakin, Richard Lansing
Dakin, Edward Saltinstall Dakin

*Miniature on ivory by George H. Hite (c. April, 1839) copied from the original
by Henry E. Huntington Gallery*

Parents

THE OLCOTTS had not been established in Cherry Valley many years before the New York Central Railroad was extended westward through the Mohawk Valley sixteen miles north of the village. And then there happened to Cherry Valley what happened to many villages in a similar situation, villages that had been on the turnpikes but were bypassed by the railroads and became isolated as the great routes of travel changed.

The opening of the Erie Canal in 1825 had been the first serious blow to through trade in the town, but the real decline now set in. Cherry Valley had reached its acme in 1815. After that Rochester and other towns on the waterways and railroad had rapidly outstripped the little village. With its great source of revenue diverted, the town dropped with remarkable suddenness from a place of leading importance to a commonplace country village. Its wealth and social standing, however, continued for another fifty years.

The final contribution to the decline of the village (and this was typical of other villages in the East, too) was the fact that many of its young people left to seek greater opportunities elsewhere. But those of its sons and daughters who made their mark in the world felt allegiance to the home of their fathers where most of them returned periodically. Although the Olcott children followed this trend and left the village, so great was their love for Cherry Valley that they never stayed away long and they always returned to "Wood-bine," which they considered home.

Egbert, the Olcotts' eldest son, was a soldier in the Civil War. He commanded the company that was raised in Cherry Valley immediately after Sumter, and engaged as Colonel and later as Brevet General with the 121st New York Volunteers in all the battles of the Army of the Potomac. He was the youngest acting Colonel in the Northern Army and the only Olcott who did not buy a substitute. When Susan Nelson of Yorktown, Virginia, heard that Northern troops were being stationed there, she vowed never to speak to one of them. But when Egbert was assigned the Nelson House as his headquarters, the beautiful young rebel, seeing him through a window, exclaimed (according to an old family story), "My God, there is my fate!" And he was. After the war he carried her north with him as his bride. But she remained a rebel. At the Mason-Dixon Line, where everyone was required to swear allegiance to the flag of the Union, she refused. The commanding officer sternly declared that for disciplinary measures she should be placed in the custody of—Col. Egbert Olcott! Some years later Egbert returned to Cherry Valley with Susan and their three young children. After Egbert's death Susan took the children to Richmond, Virginia, where they lived with her sister during the winter, returning to Cherry Valley for summers.

The second son, Horatio Leonard Olcott, served with the Navy Department in Washington during the war, then went into the brokerage business in New York. But for him, his wife, and their six children, Cherry Valley was home through all the long summers. When they filed into church there, they all had to sit down and rise at once to crowd into their pew. When little Perry was asked, "What is thy duty towards God?" he replied, "Glorify God and endure Him forever." These poor children were required to leave Sunday dinner before dessert to get to Sunday School on time. When they were little they had a nurse who used to sing them to sleep with this cheerful lullaby:

> We lay our garments by,
> Upon the bed to rest.
> Soon death will come and claim us all
> And leave our souls undressed.

The youngest Olcott daughter, Grace, married first a Cherry Valley lawyer, Frank Morse, and after his death she married Walter Campbell. Although Walter's business was in New York, the Campbells always spent their summers in Cherry Valley. The first time Grace returned to "Woodbine" with her second husband, she found that someone had hung a large crayon portrait of her first husband on the wall of her bedroom. Next morning she said, "Frank looked down so reproachfully at me that I got up and covered him with an apron." That day she gave him back to his mother.

There could be no greater contrast between two sisters than between Julia Little and Anna Maria, the older daughters; yet each represented a type of the time. Julia was the cold-bath-every-morning type, strong for women's rights and the Republican party. She married Andrew Jackson Perry, a Democrat, who was on the way to becoming Democratic candidate for mayor of New York City when she made him become a Republican! Julia was never sick and had little sympathy for those who were. The only remedies offered in her home were a bottle of "Tucker's 59" or Dr. Zolnoski's water treatment, which was very popular at the time. Although they lived in Brooklyn, where their big four-story brownstone house over- flowed with nieces and nephews through the winters, the Perrys spent their summers in Cherry Valley, as all the others did. One of her nieces recalls a scene at "Woodbine" when Andrew banged on the dinner table and declared, "Julia, when I die I order you now to have my body cremated," to which she as firmly replied, "Andrew, when you die I shall do exactly as I please with your body!"

Anna Maria, on the other hand, was beautiful, shy, and deeply religious. She thought that men were the downtrodden creatures of this world and woman's chief glory was in serving them. Caring nothing for woman suffrage, she was a homebody, a fine musician, sensitive, and gentle. Anna Maria loved social life, but she feared for her soul. She would go to dances but sit them all out, for the gaping jaws of Hell were waiting to gobble her up if she tripped the first step. But at a party one evening where the older Dakin boys were present, she weakened under the persuasions of George. For she was falling in love with him and could not resist the temptation. None of the other girls seemed to fear for their souls! So she danced. But she lay awake much of that night, experiencing the tortures of Hell in

15. September 26, 1888. Glensfoot Bend in road (above Mr. Cox's) leading to Cherry Valley from the west. Presbyterian Church spire in the distance

her imagination. Later George was able to quiet her fears, and soon after this they became engaged. She was only sixteen and quite too shy for marriage as yet. In fact she kept putting off the wedding until she had kept him waiting for almost six years.

Their devotion deepened during these years and George spent much time in Cherry Valley with Annie. When he was away their letters were frequent, and she read the many books he sent her. One they particularly enjoyed reading together was *The Life and Letters of Jean Paul Richter*. A history of Cherry Valley in speaking of George Dakin calls him "a very gentlemanly man of scholarly tastes," while another says he "stood out in startling distinction from most men of his day for his learning, his wit, and his deep love for humanity, which endeared him to everybody." At last, in the summer of 1857 Annie confided to her mother that she feared she simply could not live without George any longer. They were married that September, when she was twenty-two and he was twenty-five.

They had a formal wedding in the Presbyterian Church of which the bride's father was a deacon. The bridesmaids were led by Julia as maid of honor and little Gracie was flower girl. The reception that followed at "Woodbine" was a happy occasion for Annie until it was over and the good nights were said. Then how she wished that she and George might depart at once, but no stagecoach left the village at night. It would be hard enough to face her family and friends in the morning but doubly hard for her to go to her room now. So the shy young bride undressed in her mother's room, then wrapped herself in her grandmother's old gray shawl. But when she went to her

16. Civil War family group, the Horatio Olcott family in 1865: (l. to r.)
Anna Maria Olcott Dakin, 30; Great-grandmother Leonard, 76; Paul Worth
Dakin, 3; Grace Vernon Olcott, 15; Harriet Leonard Olcott, 51; Horatio
Josiah Olcott, 55; Horatio Leonard Olcott, 26; Leonard Dakin, 7; Julia Little
Olcott Perry, 33; Egbert Olcott, 29
Reproduced from an old print

room in this array, she was so relieved to see George feigning sleep that her shyness left her and she blessed him in her heart. How understanding he was! Gratefully she said her prayers and fell at once into a peaceful sleep.

Next day they left for Clinton, Iowa, where George had secured a position in a bank. Annie took a bridesmaid with her on their honeymoon, and she made her sit next to George in the train lest someone might guess Annie was his wife. She took a fine, big, strong Englishwoman, Mary Yendley, to be her housekeeper. "Mame" she was called.

A few months later, how thankful she was that she had Mame to comfort her. For one night she slipped downstairs to the kitchen, and crawling onto Mame's ample lap, buried her head on her shoulder, sobbing, "I am going back to Cherry Valley."

Mame comforted her a few minutes and then asked, "Does Mr. Dakin know?"

"Oh, no, he must think only that I am homesick."

So the unhappy little bride left her husband and traveled alone the long, long way back to Cherry Valley. As she had not let anyone know she was coming, no one was at the stagecoach to meet her. With her carpetbag in hand, she walked down the street to "Woodbine" and up the steps. There was her mother standing in the doorway.

"Why, Anna Maria," she exclaimed, "what has happened?"

"Oh, Mother," dissolving in tears on her shoulder, "I—I'm going to have a baby!"

17. The Presbyterian Church

of privacy (there were no curtains or divisions), and the general discomfort were too much for them. For the rest of the journey they stayed in hotels at night. Annie did the same on this trip. But one wonders how she ever made the morning trains on time, for this was long before the four standard time zones were adopted by the railroads, and there were sixty-odd different local times by which trains operated. The trip probably took her five or six days, and it was with great relief that her husband welcomed her back to Clinton.

His tenderness made it possible for her to accept the inevitable, and soon she even became proud that her baby Leonard was the first grandchild in the family. Indeed, his arrival released her suddenly from the religious bondage that made her believe the floor of Hell was paved with unbaptized babies. She said that when she looked at her innocent baby she simply knew it was not true. After that it was easy for her to take up dancing. Before she died, she was even crossing out from her Bible the Psalms she did not like, the ones she was sure David had not written!

When Lenny was two-and-a-half, Annie could wait no longer to show him to her mother. So she took him back to Cherry Valley to spend Christmas at "Woodbine," while her brother Horatio went to Clinton to keep George company. For a Christmas gift Annie sent George a lovely miniature that she had had painted of Lenny, which delighted the proud father's heart.

After remaining in Iowa a few years, George decided to move back east. Clinton had been established only two years before the Dakins went out there, but by 1859 it was a city with mule-drawn

19. Leonard Dakin,
our photographer,
at two-and-a-half
*From a miniature
painted on ivory—
artist unknown*

streetcars. The wooden sidewalks on stilts frequently floated down the river in high water, and the Dakins even experienced a disastrous flood. Much worse was a hurricane so severe as to carry the heavy church bell a block away. But chiefly, they were too far from the home ties for Annie to be completely happy. So they packed their belongings, said farewell to their first home, crossed the Mississippi by ferry, and took a train for New York.

The decade of the 1850's was a dangerous period for travel in America because of the frequency of railway accidents. Traffic by rail was swelling rapidly and velocity was increasing; the average rate of speed had jumped from twenty-five to thirty-five miles an hour. But there was no corresponding improvement in the old roadbeds, bridges, or rolling stock.* Thus it happened that as the Dakins' train was crossing a bridge of flimsy construction it gave way under them in the dark of night and one car piled on top of another in the river. Pullman sleepers were in operation then, and as the water rose to their berth they placed Lenny in an upper berth and stood in the water up to their waists until they were rescued.

After arriving safely in the East, George bought a seat on the New York Stock Exchange and established his family in Brooklyn near Sister Julia. But they built a house in Cherry Valley for the summers, and it was this they called home. They chose a site on high ground about a mile north of the village center. Because of its spacious lawns and beautiful views of the hills in every direction, they named their home "Uplawn."

*SEYMOUR DUNBAR, *A History of Travel in America* (Indianapolis: Bobbs-Merrill, 1915), p. 1054

20. "Uplawn," the Dakin home in Cherry Valley

The Family at "Woodbine"

BEFORE MANY YEARS had elapsed Lenny had a brother Paul and a little sister Florence, called Floy. Annie and George were happy to have them grow up with the other Olcott grandchildren who returned eagerly to "Woodbine" every summer.

One day Lenny was watching some carpenters as they repaired the steps to the front porch, absorbing their profane language with close attention. He was wearing his first suit with pockets in the trousers. A little later, Grandfather Olcott, standing unobserved in the open French window, was shocked to hear Lenny pour forth a string of oaths as he marched up and down the porch with his hands in his pockets. He led his grandson to an upper bedroom, where he gave him a spanking. Then he set Lenny down and told him to say his prayers. The moment the door was closed, Lenny, who was always known as the philosopher who never cried over spilt milk, flopped down to his knees and repeated as rapidly as possible, "Now I lay me down to sleep." Then he bounded down the stairs to watch the carpenters again. When Lenny had his picture taken in this special suit, although ordinarily an obedient child, he refused to take both hands out of his pockets. He agreed to compromise, though, and remove one. On another occasion, when Lenny was about to be spanked, he tried to get a lighter sentence by handing his father a piece of string and saying, "Here, Father, use this and I will cry just as hard."

By this time the Olcotts had made many changes in "Woodbine." In 1860 they had installed the first bathroom in the town. Lenny's brother Paul, at eighty-four, recalled: "I, as a little boy, was not encouraged to use it. In fact, it was generally reserved for emergencies." Ample provision for a large family was made elsewhere, a room behind the summer kitchen for the women and children and an outhouse beyond the woodshed for the men, trellised over with woodbine. Since the ladies made a social affair of the morning visit there and generally went in a group with the children, one can readily understand why provision was made for so many at once.

In the sixties and seventies it was a mark of social standing not only to have a bathroom but also to have a cooking stove in the kitchen. When the Olcotts acquired theirs, their cook felt as the cook at the White House had felt when in President Fillmore's administration the first cooking stove was installed there. She quit, saying the old-fashioned fireplace was good enough for her!

The delightful old garden at "Woodbine" with its lilac- and syringa-bordered lawn was divided by a flower-edged walk over-arched by trellised woodbine. This stretched through a spacious apple and plum orchard to a brook, whose banks were blue with forget-me-nots and over which a rustic bridge led to a centenarian oak.

In the early days the lawn was not clipped close as in these photographs, but Grandmother Olcott boasted that hers was the first

21. September 16, 1887. South side of "Woodbine": (on steps, top) Anna Maria Olcott Dakin; (bottom) Grandmother Olcott; (on porch) Julia Perry, holding little Julie, and companions

cleared lawn in Cherry Valley and that she was the first person in the village to own a lawn mower. Her garden abounded with her favorite flowers: old-fashioned roses and stately Madonna lilies. They extended the full length of the garden walk, all the way to the rustic bridge, and were such a lovely sight in full bloom that people came from many miles away to see them. Their daughter Grace kept the baptismal font at church filled with them on Sundays. When Plate 26 was shown to old Jesse Walton, whose father was the Olcotts' last gardener, he recalled that those lily bulbs were brought from England in 1846 by one Billy Farar, who guarded them with a shotgun to keep the boys from pilfering them.

For the Olcott children and grandchildren this garden was an important part of their lives. They paddled in the brook and climbed the fruit trees, and each child "owned" a special apple or plum tree. On a seat built around the great oak, yesterday merged with today as the children listened wide-eyed to the stories for which Grandfather Olcott was famous. He made the past come alive with these stories, ranging from the pioneer life of their ancestors, Puritans who landed at Plymouth and sea captains at Nantucket, to his own childhood in Hudson. He told them how his great-grandfather, a sheep farmer in Hartford, had instituted the ceremony peculiar to the Olcott family of christening each new baby the morning after its birth and feeding it with due solemnity on lamb broth. The family looked upon this ceremony as typical of their pastoral habits and love of peace.

When the stories touched on the Revolution, the children might return to the house by way of the great elm behind the barn. In 1778,

22. The Horatio Olcotts' grandchildren in 1883. Standing (l. to r.) Anna Miles
Olcott (Nannie), 15; Harriet Leonard Olcott, 11; Jackson Perry Olcott, 9;
Leonard Dakin, 25; Horatio Whiting Olcott, 12; Marion Olcott, 13; seated
(l. to r.) Paul Worth Dakin, 21; Florence Dakin, 14; Egberta Olcott, 10;
Harold Francis Morse, 6; Emma Olcott, 15; Horace Williams Olcott, 5

when it was only a sapling, an obstreperous recruit had been tied to this tree and flogged into submission. The children regarded it with some horror and called it the "flogging elm."

Inside the house, the children loved best to explore the attic. They crawled into it on their hands and knees through a tiny little door at the end of the third-floor hall. That in itself was exciting, but then they had to negotiate (and often did it head first) two very steep steps down to the attic floor, which was on a lower level. They felt a strange snugness here when raindrops pelted the attic roof noisily. And on sunny days when flies buzzed on the window panes, they liked the smell of warm wood mingled with that of sage and other herbs drying on sheets on the floor. Among the relics in the attic were dusty old whale-oil lamps and hoop skirts hanging on nails. The children dressed up in old dresses with fluted ruffles bound with velvet and their Aunt Grace's postage-stamp hats, rather like old English soldiers' caps, which always looked as if they were hung on the side of the head and made one wonder what kept them on.

They loved to rummage through the old soldier's traveling box in which Uncle Egbert's Civil War epaulets and belt were kept, still as bright as gold. His cap and sword were there, too, the scabbard with a bullet hole in it. But the most prized relic was a captured flag. The children were not allowed to touch it, and it was not until some years later that they learned its touching story and one of them actually became a part of that story. It seems that the ladies of Savannah, Georgia, had embroidered in gold a red silk banner for the Savannah Volunteer Guards. There was an altar with golden flowers

23. Lenny Dakin at seven wearing his first suit with pockets
From a daguerreotype

and the inscription, "Our Altars and Our Firesides." This banner Egbert captured after fierce fighting; but he so admired the gallant spirit and valiant fighting of the young Southerners that when he gave the banner to his wife he asked her to return it to Savannah if she ever found the chance. After Egbert died she found that only three of the original Savannah Volunteer Guards were living. She got in touch with them and during a Georgia celebration she returned the banner in her son Horatio's name. In appreciation they sent the boy a double-backed gold watch with an inscription inside stating the occasion.

This attic had a steep, narrow staircase that wound down into Great-grandmother Leonard's room below and was dark and difficult to go either up or down in a hurry. Much easier were the straight, wide stairs leading to the servants' attic from the back kitchen. There was a kind of unearthly fascination about visiting the private quarters of Isabel, the cook. This was done only on personal invitation. Isabel had once had a husband who, when Daguerreotypes were at their height of popularity, had promised to have his "likeness" made as a gift for his wife, but he died before fulfilling this promise. Isabel, not to be outwitted by his death, had a portrait made of him as he lay in his coffin. It was this picture, large and glittering on her bureau, that held the children spellbound.

We have no pictures of the upstairs rooms at "Woodbine" and only one interior view downstairs. Plate 27 shows the double parlors, as they were called, high-ceilinged rooms, spacious and formal, with long gilt-framed mirrors at each end giving the appear-

24. "Woodbine" garden from rear: Presbyterian Church on left, "flogging elm" at right

children's slidings, which were made something of an adventure by the sharp curve halfway down. Then there were the usual hatrack, umbrella stand, and stiff chairs, and, in later years, a great pipe that went up from the furnace through the hall to the floor above. Across the hall was the sitting room, or library. This room was the heart of family life. In the bay window Grandmother Olcott rocked the little children in her arms and sang them her favorite old songs.

Plate 28 shows the Olcott family—children, grandchildren, and horses—at the time of Horatio and Harriet's fifty-fifth wedding anniversary. Horatio has been president of the bank now for thirty-two years. His wife still calls him "Mr. Olcott," but to him she is just "Hat." These family occasions were jubliant, especially the fiftieth anniversary when the children twined the banisters with goldenrod and hung a great bell of tansey in the hall. All wore badges of yellow ribbon and there were lovely gifts, including a gold thimble for Grandmother Olcott and a gold-headed cane for Grandfather.

The three Olcott horses were as much a part of the family as any of the other members. There was always a skittish pair of Canadian ponies called Hector and Paris, the individual ponies changing with time but the names remaining. The classical revival that influenced the naming of the towns of Rome, Ithaca, Syracuse, Utica, and scores of others influenced even the naming of horses in Cherry Valley. The dapple-gray Hector and Paris had recently been replaced by the black Hector and Paris in this picture, very spirited, handsome, and hardy. And there was always a third pony called Helen of Troy, especially for Grandmother Olcott's use with the

26. July 16, 1888. Emma Olcott (foreground) admires Madonna lilies at "Woodbine"

buggy or phaeton. Later a cousin, who must have been a member of the S.P.C.A., presented the family with a horse named Homer on condition that they would not dock its tail.

The author can recall that whenever, as a little girl, she happened to be at "Woodbine" when Helen of Troy was fastened to the hitching post, she always asked Grandmother to take her for a drive. She was never refused, and they always drove down the Plank Road, but only as far as the Old Toll Gate. There the child was perfectly content to turn around because—they would have to pay a penny to go through!

Among the happiest memories of the Olcott grandchildren are the many drives they took with their grandparents. One day it might be an expedition to gather wild plums which grew abundantly along the roadsides, the ground beneath the trees frequently being covered with fallen fruit. After they had carefully filled their baskets in anticipation of the delicious plum butter to follow, or gathered buckets of wild black cherries for cherry bounce, they would gather around for stories.

Grandmother might tell them of how Mr. Dunlop had changed the original name of the village, Lindesay's Bush, to Cherry Valley, for this wild fruit, which was so much more plentiful in the early days. Or she might tell them about the distinguished lawyer, Levi Beardsley, president of the state Senate, who took a guest of national importance on a foxhunt one day. Hot and thirsty after the chase, he pulled a flask from his pocket and offered his guest some refreshment, only to find to his utter exasperation that it was filled with

27. Double parlors at "Woodbine," with painting of Priscilla Alden on easel

water. "That was some of Elizabeth's work!" he said in disgust. But Elizabeth was a maternal wife who knew what was good for him.

Whenever they drove across the Old Iron Bridge they paused to hear the favorite story of why Joe Tucker gave his wife a whipping. Joe had told her there were two things she should never lend. One was the fine comb, the other was the darning needle. But she did lend the darning needle to a little girl who, in crossing this very bridge, let it fall between the planks into the creek below. So Mrs. Joe got a whipping for her disobedience!

Grandfather often took the children fishing in the Cherry Valley Creek, where they caught bull heads, dace, and suckers. When Lenny Dakin was about ten he caught the biggest sucker anyone could remember. As they baited their hooks they talked about the Indians who had fished in this same stream. From time immemorial they had used a narrow winding trail through the wilderness from the Mohawk at Canajoharie to the headwaters of the Susquehanna, and as the Cherry Valley Creek was the farthest-reaching branch of that river, it was at this very spot where the children fished that the Indians launched their canoes to pass on to Pennsylvania and the Chesapeake for war or hunting.

After the first white settlers came, all the region southwest of Canajoharie was vaguely known as Cherry Valley, and Otsego Lake was called Cherry Valley Lake. The trail that followed the Cherry Valley Creek south through the valley, the earliest thoroughfare on this frontier, was worn a foot deep by generations of moccasined feet. In time it was made passable for vehicles when half of it was paved

28. The Olcott family assembled at "Woodbine" to celebrate Horatio and Harriet's fifty-fifth wedding anniversary in 1886

with planks, and it was known as the Old Plank Road. Piles of planks were stacked here and there along the roadside for use in frequent replacement. When these were stacked as in a log cabin, the children loved to climb down inside the piles to play.

Of course, no picnics or drives were permitted on Sunday, when everyone went to church. Great-grandmother Leonard, Harriet's mother, never missed a service, but she had to eat caraway seeds throughout the sermon to keep awake. Harold, the most restless of the grandchildren, found it very hard to sit still in church and sometimes slipped down under the pews, where he crawled around on his hands and knees looking for lost pennies or dimes. One Sunday when he was fascinating the other children by catching flies, Mr. Swinnerton, the minister, interrupted the service by demanding sternly, "Keep that child quiet!" But Harold really disgraced the family when he took some bread from the Communion plate, tearfully explaining later, "But I was hungry!" The same child once said to his mother, "There is never any dust on Grandmudder's Bible, but look at the dust on yours." One day he put his hands behind his back, shook his head, and refused to be kissed by a visitor. "Why, most little boys like to be kissed by ladies," she said. And he replied, "Little boys like I are don't." Once when he held a cow's swishing tail for his cousin Horace, who liked to milk, neither boy could understand why the milk stopped coming.

Every spring nomadic gypsies camped in Flint's Woods east of the village. The gypsy women, in their bright colored outfits with beads and bangles and great gold hoops in their ears, brought a flutter

29. September 17, 1887. Grandmother Olcott and companion in her phaeton leaving "Woodbine"

to the hearts of the girls when they made the rounds of the village and told the fortunes of anyone who would cross their palms with a bit of silver. The children were warned to keep away from the gypsies, but young Horace Olcott, the most adventuresome of the grandsons, was ready with a carefully laid plan when they came one spring. Early in the morning he went alone to the gypsies' camp, carrying in a burlap bag two hens, whose legs he had tied together, and all his savings for the past year. With these he succeeded in making a deal that rejoiced his heart, for he became the proud owner of a ratty little pony, which he called Coxey. To be sure, his grandfather made him work to pay for the hens he had taken from the chicken yard and he had to prove to his anxious mother that Coxey had no designs on his life even though he could go like the wind.

Plate 33 shows Horace in an old-fashioned hammock. About this time he became the hero of so famous a Cherry Valley story that it made the *New York Tribune* and the *Albany Herald*. It was called "The Rooster Case." Many of the town boys owned fighting cocks and Horace aspired to own one, too, in spite of his parents' objections. One must admit that he was subjected to well-nigh irresistible temptation by living next door to the Park House, whose proprietor, Mr. Jensen, bred these birds.

Finally he saved up the necessary few dollars and purchased a young game cock from Mr. Jensen. Since it was Horace's special chore to feed the chickens that summer, no one noticed when an extra rooster was added to the lot. That it was a fighter must be kept strictly secret; only his cousin Harold Morse knew. After Horace

30. September 24, 1888. Old Plank Road, with its fork to Cooperstown via Middlefield. Planks at left for repair of road

clipped his comb and gills, the two boys would chase him around every day to harden him up and improve his wind. One day Horace even let him have a brush with an old rooster of the barnyard type whose spurs had been filed blunt and could not injure him. When it was full-grown the boys would slip out after supper with the cock and put it to the test behind Oliver's Grocery Store. So good a fighter did it become that it soon began to attract the attention of the towns-people.

The morning after one particularly successful fight, witnessed by a dozen or more men and boys, a fight in which the cock was blinded in one eye, Horace found it missing from the coop. For some time he could get no clue as to who had stolen it. Finally a rumor reached Horace that if he wanted to recover his cock he must go up to the shack of old Peg-leg Nelson and his son Beany in the quarry.

With no thought of the illegal aspect of his action, he jumped on the back of Coxey and rode madly up to the shack. There he found his rooster tied by the leg to a stake. That alone was evidence that it did not belong there. Horace cut the cord, but as he started out of the yard with the bird under his arm, old Peg-leg Nelson came hobbling after him shouting, "I will have the law on ye!"

Imagine the consternation in the Olcott household when a few days later the town constable appeared at "Woodbine" to arrest young Horace with a warrant charging him with petty larceny! The family saw him hauled before a Justice of the Peace, where he was held in two-hundred-dollar bail. His father and grandfather refused to pay it. Let him suffer the consequences of his own misdeeds. But his

31. Old Toll Gate
Photo by A. Jay Thompson

uncle, George Dakin, took compassion on him and furnished the two hundred dollars without consulting the others.

At that time a well-known Pittsburgh lawyer, Mr. Robb, who happened to be vacationing at the Park House, volunteered to take Horace's case. When Horace told him how the bird was tied to a stake on the Nelson place and how, when he rode up to his own barn and threw him in among the other chickens, he ran immediately to the food trough and began to eat, Mr. Robb said, "Enough! We are ready for trial."

In the earlier days lawsuits had been such a source of entertainment in the Cherry Valley district that sessions of the court were held in the evenings for the enjoyment of all, and before the trial opened it was incumbent upon each contestant to treat the crowd. Times were somewhat changed now, but this suit brought echoes of the past when it produced such merriment in the village that for several days the stores were closed so that everyone might attend the hearing.

When Mr. Robb simply played cat and mouse with the plaintiff's local attorney, that gentleman complained that it was "no fair to run him up against a city lawyer" and that the defense had "brought so many people in to try to influence the court." He opened his case with a long dissertation on the defendant, whose father and grandfather were known to him "as among our most respected citizens, but what a problem the defendant must be to them! Only recently he had been riding in a horse race in the cemetery with no respect for the dead!"

When Horace took the witness chair he had in his arms the

32. Old iron bridge across Cherry Valley Creek, Harriott house in the background

rooster as Exhibit A. The bird fluttered and squawked to the great annoyance of the judge but delight of the crowd.

"Keep that bird quiet," the judge shouted to Horace, startling the poor child so as he pointed his finger at him that Horace dropped the rooster, which ran squawking all over the courtroom before it could be caught. Heads were bumped against heads and two boys were knocked to the floor as they tried to help, amidst shouts of "Here he is!" or "Now we've got him!" until the place was in an uproar.

When quiet was finally regained Horace testified that the scraggy appearance of the rooster's tail was due to the fact that the plaintiff had pulled out some of his brown tail feathers so that he might not be recognized. When the judge asked, "How many brown tail feathers did the rooster have in his tail?" the crowd became so convulsed with laughter that it was difficult to restore order. Indeed, one of the guests from "Uplawn" laughed so unrestrainedly that the judge asked her to leave the courtroom.

In questioning the witnesses for the prosecution, Mr. Robb brought out that they did not know the breed of the rooster or its age. They seemed to know only that it was owned by Beany Nelson, but they could not support this contention. With this Mr. Robb rested his case.

The witnesses for the defense included poor little white-faced Harold Morse, frightened but loyal as he corroborated every statement his cousin Horace had made, and Mr. Jensen, a blunt but taciturn old gentleman, who was annoyed at being called away from

33. July 30, 1890. Group on lawn with Horace Olcott of the "rooster case" in hammock

his hotel. When asked how he knew that the particular rooster which he had sold to young Olcott when half-grown was the same rooster that was here in court, he shouted at the judge, "How do I know my own children?"

After a very brief summing up by Mr. Robb, in which he clearly indicated that any decision by the judge other than an acquittal would disqualify him as capable of deciding on questions of law, Horace was acquitted and Cherry Valley's most famous trial ended.

A seasonal activity that delighted the Olcott grandchildren was hop-picking. (In Plates 3 and 36 the set-up poles of a hop-yard are visible, and in Plate 35, the poles as they are stacked after the picking was done.) This was a time of great merriment, when alarm clocks were set for rising with the dawn. The farmers sent big springless lumber wagons around early in the morning to collect the pickers, who sat facing each other on two long boards. The girls wore coverall aprons, sunbonnets or big straw hats, and coarse cotton gloves for protection from sun and insects while picking the hops. Singing and storytelling were part of the fun, and they picnicked for lunch, making a full day of it. One day was usually enough at a time for the girls, and some older member of the family was ordinarily with them lest they come in too close contact with the migrant city pickers who flooded into the country for this work. They regarded the whole thing as a lark and laughed and waved as they came clattering home at night, when they were hailed, "Dirty hop-pickers! Dirty hop-pickers!" in a singsong voice by all the people they passed on the way.

34. July 17, 1890. Group with Harold Morse and Horace Olcott, witnesses for the defense

But one day was not enough for the boys. In fact, Horace's activities began in the spring in the Snyder hop-yard when he joined his friend Jo Snyder and others who were hired to "tie hops." Since the boys were too short to reach the high stragglers that must be curled sunwise along the twine from pole to pole, Mr. Snyder let them ride into the yard and stand on their horses' backs at each pole to reach the vines. A few lumps of sugar were enough to make Coxey cooperate. In the fall the boys took the hop-picking more seriously than the girls did and often picked two or three boxes a day (at fifty cents a box). They considered it an easy way to earn a little money, and it was good fun.

Hop-picking may have been seasonal, but teasing their dear old grandfather was perennial fun for the grandchildren. Knowing that he disliked Lydia Pinkham and her "pink pills for pale people," the boys would cut her picture out of the paper and stick it up where he could not help seeing it. Lenny Dakin, burlesquing Gilbert and Sullivan, even made up a rollicking verse about that beneficent lady and her pink pills.

As you can see in Plate 28, Grandfather Olcott's hair was rather long and curly. Knowing that his hair was his secret pride, his wife humored him by putting it up in curl papers every night. They used sheets of toilet paper for this rite, and one must smile at the picture of the old gentleman, assisted by his young daughter Gracie, smoothing out for reuse any untorn sheets and placing them beside the comb in readiness every evening. One Sunday morning something interrupted their preparations for church and Grandfather appeared in the

35. September 24, 1888. Old Plank Road with hop poles stacked at right

family pew with half the curl papers still in. His grandchildren never let him forget that occasion!

In his advancing years cataracts grew over his eyes. Taking advantage of his dimming sight one day, a few hours after a mouse had been seen running across the room, Harold put his felt pen wiper with a stuffed mouse on top on the floor. Exclaiming, "There's the mouse again, Grandfather!" he nearly burst with laughter as Horatio whacked at the thing with his cane. But they did not laugh the time he knocked over the bottle of ink on the rug because he did not see it or when he served the first ladle of soup onto the tablecloth. Then it was time for the cataract operation, and their hearts were all lighter when it proved a perfect success.

So much did the children enjoy having him with them that when a picnic was afoot, or an expedition to go nutting, they would send someone up to the bank to hurry him home and promise to wait for him. Then they would watch eagerly for the loved figure with the cape flowing from his shoulders to come around the corner. On these picnics, in his later years, they would arrange the seat cushions from the carriage on the ground for him to have a nap and tenderly cover him with the carriage robe.

But it was not only his grandchildren whose hearts he warmed. He was so loved and respected in Cherry Valley that an old neighbor once said that when she met him and he spoke to her "it was like a benediction."

36. Start of Plank Road between Cherry Valley and Roseboom, and Cherry Valley Creek, where Grandfather Olcott fished with his grandchildren

The Dakins at "Uplawn"

As THE GRANDCHILDREN grew into their teens, the center of their activities shifted frequently from "Woodbine" to "Uplawn." Here, too, there was a large garden and a barn with chickens, a cow, and three horses. It was in the big storeroom over the carriage house that George and Anna's grandson Herbert found his father Leonard's glass-plate negatives of these photographs many years later.

In Plate 38 we see the barn and dear old Mame, the housekeeper who had accompanied Annie on her wedding trip to Iowa, and Terry Lynch, the Dakins' faithful man. When George first engaged him, fresh from Ireland, Terry told him in playful exaggeration, "Begorra, Mr. Dakin, everybody in Ireland knows about you!" And he used to tell the children, "Sure and the bees in Ireland are as big as the sheep in this country." If one of the children had a cold, Terry would present him with a fat stick of licorice candy in the shape of a large teaspoon as a remedy. Naturally all the children loved him.

Since the seven bedrooms at "Uplawn" were not enough for all the guests who overflowed the house constantly, the Dakins built a guest cottage across the lawn. There they had a billiard room and later Leonard's photographic darkroom.

"Uplawn" was furnished for the most part in the typical mode of the late Victorian era. As the seventies showed an increasing taste for oriental rugs, there are a few here, scattered over the nailed-down matting on the floors. There were also a few rugs of animal skins, which the family sometimes used on the lawn (see Plate 94). Evidently the oriental rugs were carried out to the lawn, too, for we see them in Plates 93, 105, and 118.

Amidst the combination of wicker and upholstered furniture are the customary what-nots, portieres, antimacassars, and a silk-and-lace petticoat draping the lampshade on the center table, itself adorned with a ball-fringed plush cover. Four kerosene lamps on brackets swing in the opening beside the sliding doors (there were twenty-six of these lamps to be trimmed and filled every morning); a crocheted duster bag hangs under one of these lamps; and an embroidered "throw" gracefully adorns the easel that displays a colorful painting by I. M. Gulderhouse.

The books on the parlor table are not the gift-book variety bound in tooled leather that were a sign of the times, for this was a family of readers. Large paintings by members of the Hudson River School hang over the black marble mantel and over the scarf-draped piano, which is littered with bric-a-brac and photographs. A small profile portrait of a Dakin ancestor, other smaller oil paintings, and marble busts decorate the parlor and library. Large steel engravings hang on the walls in the dining room, including two not visible in these photographs by Sir Edwin Landseer, with his inevitable stags.

Over the fireplace and the pier glass in the library are great plumes of pampas grass from Florida, where the Dakins regularly wintered. Beside the fireplace a large bow of ribbon gives a touch of

37. September 4, 1888. Guests around south porch at ''Uplawn''

"charm" to the wicker wood basket, beside which lies the conch that the children pressed to their ears to hear the ocean roar. Another shell hangs by the doorway to the library and a Japanese scroll hangs on the wall nearby.

Several flower arrangements are visible, notably the one on a stand by the piano in a quaint little two-story flower vase, but the large rubber plant from Florida which stands in one corner of the room does not show in these pictures.

The heavy wool cover on the reading table in the library differs only in material from the flower-stamped plush cover that usually replaced the white linen on the dining room table between meals. In the library we see the top of a large square footstool done in fine needlepoint by Anna Maria, with a reclining dog in the center worked in colored beads on a white ground.

Upstairs great black-walnut beds reared their backs to the ceilings in the spare rooms, known as "the red room," "the blue room," and so on. We have no pictures to show the gay Japanese fans pinned to the walls in Floy's room, where tie-back curtains made a canopy over her corner dressing table. Each bedroom of course was provided with a washstand set, the one in Floy's room decorated with a pattern of pink rosebuds, as befitting a young girl.

One bathroom served the entire family. Its zinc-lined tub of black walnut had a great tank of water overhead, which was pumped full daily from the three huge cisterns in the cellar. An outhouse at the barn was used by the servants and by the men of the household when there were guests. The young ladies of that day were so modest that when two were rooming together each one would pour the hot water she had fetched from the bathroom into her basin and proceed to bathe in the most awkward manner under her nightgown, lest her roommate catch a glimpse of her anatomy. Then into the sleeves of her gown she would pop her arms again, set the basin on the floor, and finish her bath by washing her feet in it.

All the girls in the family learned to sew, and Ella, young Horatio's wife, was their favorite teacher because no one else in the world could make such exquisite doll clothes as she. Ella is the center figure in Plate 44, which shows five women sewing in the parlor at "Uplawn." She used to help the little girls make outfits for their dolls to match their own, so that sewing became a pleasure for them.

Both she and Grandmother Olcott kept great rolls of pieces of material from every dress they had, starting with their trousseaux. The pieces were cut in squares, sewn together in a long string, and each square had sewn across its corners the trimmings that had been on the dress. Calicoes and heavy silks, three or four big rolls in all, were kept in a bag hanging on a nail in Grandmother Olcott's prayer closet. These the little girls were given to unroll and examine for their amusement, and they never tired of choosing their favorites or of imagining the gowns they represented. But when they were finished with them they had to roll them up again very carefully and put them back in the prayer closet.

It was Ella whose mother had pierced her ears when she was a little girl by running a darning needle through the lobe with a cork held firmly behind it. She cried so when the first one was done that it took some urging before she would consent to have the other one done. But with this vivid memory of her own experience, she would not permit her daughters to have their ears pierced, even though it was very much the style, and thus no earrings are visible in these photographs.

"Uplawn" was closed during the winters when the children were little and the family was living in Brooklyn. But Lenny loved Cherry Valley so much that when he was six he was allowed to spend the winter at "Woodbine" with his grandparents, where he loved to "help" the men bring in the apples from the orchard and store them in barrels in the cool cellar. Here he went to school and he wrote his mother, "I read in First Reader now, not in the Primer any more."

In Brooklyn both Lenny and Paul went to the Polytechnic Institute and later were sent to the Misses Perrys' School for Boys in Glens Falls. Schoolboys of today would no doubt laugh at the submissiveness of these boys to parental authority. Lenny had promised his mother to read a chapter from the Bible to Paul every night before they went to bed. He hated doing it, especially when Paul got into bed for the reading and promptly went to sleep. But he did it faithfully, reading each chapter through to the last word while Paul slept on. And Paul, in a letter to his father, even asks permission "to have a little fight with a boy to settle a little difficulty. You won't object, I am shure [sic]."

In the summers at "Uplawn," while Annie was home caring for baby Floy, George often took the boys hunting or on long walks over the hills. Lenny was roaming the countryside alone one day when

40. "Uplawn" parlor. An embroidered "throw" adorns the easel

because "girls have no use for algebra but they can't be too well grounded in simple arithmetic."

Floy was sent to Hollins Institute (now Hollins College) in Virginia where she was a "parlor boarder," as those girls were called who took only a few courses. This reflected her mother's Victorian attitude toward the weaker sex. Girls of refinement were fragile creatures to be sheltered and protected until marriage but never to do real work. In fact, Annie's ideas were well described by Amy Reed in the *Century Magazine* for October, 1915, where she tells us that women in the sixties and seventies were constitutionally weak, helpless, and dependent. Delicacy was their chief characteristic, the visible sign of great moral sensitiveness, purity, and an ethereal, spiritual nature.

Annie also clung stubbornly to a belief in unreasonable "sayings," and with a dominating will amazing in so gentle a person, she impressed these on her children and grandchildren. To their dying day they would never eat a piece of fruit at night, for "fruit in the morning is golden, at noon is silver, but at night is lead." And her little daughter looked with envious eyes on her brothers as they sprinkled their baked potatoes liberally with pepper, which she never dared touch herself because "pepper puts boys on their horses but girls in their grave!" Floy never questioned the wisdom of her mother's decisions, not even when she longed for pink ribbons in her corset covers such as the other girls had. Yet warmth and tender affection could exist between them despite this authoritarian atmosphere.

41. "Uplawn" parlor (viewed from library), with its wicker chairs and straw matting

In Floy's blind obedience to her parents the chasm between the generations is most evident. That chasm has been bridged today by a slackening of the reins and a sense of closer companionship. It was so hard for Annie to allow her daughter to grow up that until Floy reached the age of eighteen her mother required her to go to bed at nine o'clock.

After George's early death from a heart attack, when Floy had to assume responsibility for the household during her mother's complete collapse, Annie received an almost unbelievable shock. For Floy, maturing rapidly with this new experience, suddenly took her life into her own hands and declared that she was going to become a trained nurse. Victorian attitudes and habits of mind were grooved so deeply in most of the family that Annie was not alone in being utterly horrified at this idea. They argued and tried to dissuade, but Floy stood firm. It took a strong, determined spirit to battle the family's objections, but she won her goal. Not only did she have a successful career, but she wrote a textbook, *Simplified Nursing*, that recently went into its seventh edition. Of course, as time passed and Annie adjusted herself to the new situation, she became very proud of Floy's achievements.

Many years before all this happened, when Floy was still an obedient little girl and her big brothers were in boarding school or college, there was one season of the year that remained all her life one of her happiest memories. Through their school years all the Olcott grandchildren used to spend many of their Christmas holidays in Cherry Valley. Floy loved to coast down the hill from "Uplawn"

42. "Uplawn" parlor and library, with a silk-and-lace petticoat draped over the shade of the kerosene lamp

to the barn below or to dodge the snowballs as the boys built forts on the lawn and had pitched battles. Her father helped her roll great snowballs and make and dress a fat snowman, and she learned to skate on Campbell's pond across Kilfoil's hopyard beyond the "Uplawn" garden. Sometimes at "Woodbine" a merry group of sixteen at table might force Grandfather Olcott to pound on the table for silence before he could say the blessing. And after dinner he and Grandmother Olcott would listen with deep pleasure when the children gathered around the piano to sing the familiar carols and his favorite old Scottish ballads. Or after a jolly sleigh ride on a crisp moonlit night, they would gather around a blazing fire at "Uplawn" for a hot drink while George read Dickens' *Christmas Carol* aloud to them. These memories were cherished by all the children as they returned to their various schools.

Paul Dakin was graduated from Hamilton College in 1884, but a serious illness prevented Leonard from finishing at Worcester. When his doctor prescribed outdoor work for him, his father bought property at Georgetown on the St. John's River in Florida and established Leonard there. During the next ten years he developed a large orange grove on a plantation that he called "Racimo." In the early eighties George Dakin's health forced him to retire from business, "for a period of rest," his doctor said. (Later, when old Grandfather Olcott died, George became president of the bank in Cherry Valley until his own death.) Then George, Annie, and Floy joined Leonard for winters at "Racimo."

About this time Leonard became interested in photography.

43. "Uplawn" dining room (facing parlor)

He left his grove in the summers in charge of his faithful overseer, Willie Babbitt, and returned with his family to "Uplawn" in what Harriet Beecher Stowe called "The Happy Valley," where he had the leisure to indulge his new interest and to experiment with his camera.

44. Sewing in the parlor at ''Uplawn'': (l. to r.) Anna Maria Olcott Dakin,
Harriet Leonard Olcott, Ella Jackson Olcott, Julia Olcott Perry, Florence Dakin
(at seventeen)

PART TWO

Summers in the Happy Valley, 1880-1890

Buggy Rides

IN THE 1880's the matter of chaperons was a great concern to society in the cities, but there was constant resistance in the country to this restraint of liberty. Society in the small towns was relatively untouched by the rise and fall of the chaperon. When the children, who loved to drive with their grandparents, grew into adolescence and loved to drive with each other, no objection was made by their elders, and the horse-and-buggy drive became the popular sport for sweethearts. Those were happy days indeed, when the emphasis in driving was no longer on storytelling or visiting sites of local history, but every girl went driving with her beau. And what more lovely country could they have had to drive in!

The horses at "Uplawn" were a white horse called Colonel, a wild-mannered steed called Rosinante, Pansy, whose gentle name belied her tendency to run away, and Oscar Wilde, a large, fleabitten horse who acted more or less demented whenever it rained, when he always insisted on backing up and hanging his tongue out of his mouth.

Since the horses were in constant use by both old and young, different types of carriages were needed for different occasions, from the one-seated buggy, the phaeton, the two-seated surrey either open or with the fringe on top, to the two- or three-seated democrat.

Some of these carriages, such as the stage shown in Plate 51, had rubber flaps rolled up at the sides to let down in the rain. This carried passengers from Cherry Valley to the New York Central in Canajoharie. The bearded stage driver was typical. When large parties for Otsego Lake or elsewhere more than filled these carriages, sometimes a big four-seated carryall from the livery stable was engaged and one of the boys in the party drove.

The big steppingstone and the hitching post seen in these pictures were long since removed when the horseless carriage rendered them useless. There are no rubber-tired wheels here, but in the phaeton the mudguard can be seen, following the curve of the back wheels which are larger than the front ones.

Often their drives took them to churches in neighboring towns for strawberry festivals, where they devoured strawberry shortcake and brought home wild strawberries and fresh young wintergreen shoots. Or their drives took them to the country hotels for supper parties. Around Glensfoot Bend they would drive (see Plate 15) and on to Feathers Hotel (Plate 53) in East Springfield, locally called "Four Corners" because these four corners are all there are to the town. If it happened to be in the hop-picking season Mr. Feathers would produce the fiddler who played for the hop-pickers, and the supper guests would dance while waiting for their meal to be served.

Across from the hotel stands the village store, before which a saddle horse is fastened to the hitching post. There the farmers gathered around the potbellied stove or swung their heels from the traditional cracker barrel and pickled-herring keg while the owner

45. Paul Dakin (on "Uplawn" porch) and companion (at fence) watch as
George and Anna Maria Dakin and Grandmother Olcott set out for a drive

sold his customers everything from bacon to shoe laces. The party from Cherry Valley would water their horses at the trough in the center of the square before starting for home.

The front view of Casler's Hotel at Springfield Center shows two of their carriages parked at the door and under the shed. In the view of the quite proper looking party waiting on the back porch of Casler's for the call to supper (Plate 56), there is not a sign to indicate that it was here at this very party that Leonard Dakin won a kiss in a bet that would eventually win him the lovely Jessie Messmore for his bride.

When the party finally sat down to a bountiful repast inside, one of the boys smacked his lips as he looked over the table heaped high and remarked, "Well, there are no flies on *this* supper!" The landlady gave them a jolt by replying, "I tried hard to get them all off." Meals served at these country inns were simple but generous and good and the price was twenty-five cents.

Much more elaborate and delicious dinners were enjoyed at the bigger hotels along Otsego Lake, the "Glimmerglass" of Cooper's *Leatherstocking Tales*. Here for a fixed price of $1.50 a plate they had soup, fish, roast, entrée, flapjacks, four vegetables, five relishes, three kinds of pie, ice-cream, and of course tea, coffee, and cheese. Freshly caught lake trout was a specialty always in demand. At these bigger hotels the entrée was game, but at the small country inns it was usually pork and beans. Blackstrap, a certain punch of innocent seductiveness, which was sold from casks in every country store, was served at most of these hotels. It was made of rum and molasses and

46. September 24, 1888. Leonard photographs Jessie Messmore on a drive down the valley (viewed from hill below Mr. Roseboom's, Windmill Hill in distance)

whatever, but in a more refined form it was one of Mr. Tunnicliff's specialties at Five Mile Point House.

But by no means did their drives always end at hotels for meals. They had a passion for picnics. There were picnics all the time at any time of day. Perhaps the lake was the favorite spot for these picnics, for there they could row and sail and enjoy the eighteen-mile steamer trip around the lake. Under the "picnic oak" (Plate 58) you can see the rocks where they built their fire, but fortunately you cannot smell the sulphur matches with which they had to light it.

They never went swimming on these lake picnics. Perhaps it was the dressing problem (then a more complicated procedure than today) that made them reserve this sport for the camping periods, when they would engage a cottage for a week or two and take Aunt Julia along to manage the party. To us it seems a bit whimsical to go sailing in a frock coat and a derby hat, but these gay young blades in Plate 60 were dressed *à la mode*.

Of all the pictures Plate 63 shows best what a passion picnics were with the entire family. Here is a picnic at the lake. In the group at the left are four generations: now Great-grandmother Olcott, aged eighty, Anna Maria Dakin, her son Leonard, and his three-month-old baby. It must have taken them three hours to drive to this picnic and three hours to drive home again, but neither the youngest nor the oldest was left out.

The photograph of a breakfast picnic (Plate 64) was taken on a cloudy morning with an exposure of thirteen seconds. The scene is at the head of Tekaharawa Falls on the old Seneca Trail from

47. Jessie Messmore (front) takes Maria Campbell and a friend for a drive on Old Plank Road

the Mohawk to the Susquehanna Valley, and just beyond the group of pretty girls is a drop of 180 feet into a beautiful ravine. This has been a favorite picnic spot for the youth of three generations.

When some of the younger children joined the older ones on a picnic, they were not overlooked. Plate 65 shows a group of them after their picnic is over, being read to by their newly married aunt, Grace Olcott Campbell.

Windmill Hill, the lovely mountain to the north of the valley, is seen here across the meadows. Their picnics might be in a different spot every day, but always there would be enchanting views of "The Happy Valley."

48. July 23, 1890. Grandmother Harriet Olcott stops in phaeton to chat with her daughter Anna Maria and Emma Olcott

49. August 28, 1890. The two-seated democrat had rubber curtains and used two horses

50. Anna Maria Dakin and Jessie Messmore about to board a three-seated surrey for Tunnicliff's at Five Mile Point on Otsego Lake

51. Anna Maria Dakin (with black bow) watches friends board stage for Canajoharie

56. Supper party on the porch of Casler House

57. Dinner group at "Rose Lawn" on Otsego Lake: Julia Perry (with umbrella, center), Jessie Messmore (third from right in trio at tree stump), and others

58. August 6, 1888. Picnicking at Otsego Lake. Paul (in boat), Leonard (second from left), Jessie (reading)

59. August 6, 1888. Relaxing after the picnic. Leonard and Jessie seated beside each other near tree, Paul sprawling in striped blazer

60. September 4, 1887. The boys sailed in frock coat and derby hat!

61. June 11, 1887. Picnickers watch steamer on Otsego Lake from above Watkins' Landing

62. September 2, 1886. Five Mile Point, Otsego Lake

63. September 1, 1890. Four generations picnicking at Five Mile Point, Otsego Lake: Harriet Olcott holding her great-grandson Roland Dakin, Anna Maria Dakin beside her son Leonard, Jessie third from right (seated on grass), George Dakin by tree

64. August 9, 1890. Breakfast picnic at Tekaharawa Falls: (l. to r.) Ruth
Greenleaf, Eloise Bennett, Elise Olcott, Paul Dakin, and Floy Dakin

65. Grace Olcott Campbell reading aloud to the children after a picnic at Harriott Farm. Windmill Hill in the distance

Games

THE HAPPY MEMORIES of the young people of the eighties are largely associated with the home. Both "Woodbine" and "Uplawn" overflowed with guests the entire summer. Indeed, Anna Maria Dakin had three ruling passions: hospitality, music, and religion, and each one supported the others. She always had guests; she saw to it that the guests were musical; and if any guest spilled a drop on the tablecloth, he had to cover it with a coin for her missionary box that always stood on the sideboard!

There was a patterned, familiar rhythm to those happy summer days that made unconsciously for a sense of well-being and security. The order of the day at "Uplawn" was: morning prayers, on time; breakfast at nine, with oatmeal and applesauce on week days, creamed codfish on toast on Sundays, and every day Mame's famous raised rolls; after breakfast, always music and sometimes dancing, followed by tennis. In the afternoon there was more tennis, driving and picnics, usually dancing in the evening, charades and amateur dramatics, or reading aloud.

Since the home had not yet been invaded by the phonograph or the radio, people made their own music; and at "Uplawn" it was music of such rare quality that people drove for many miles to enjoy one of Mrs. Dakin's morning musicales. Frequently among her guests were gifted musicians and singers. Together they played symphonies in duet form; they enjoyed part singing of the current light operas, especially Gilbert and Sullivan. Often George Dakin would read Shakespeare's *Midsummer Night's Dream* aloud, as his wife played Mendelssohn's music for it.

The two amusing flashlights of a group in the library are poor pictures, partly because the flash (a powder set off in a tin pan) is reflected in the pier glass and partly because there are defects in the negatives; but one wonders what the joke was that set them off so merrily. In the flashlight in the parlor (Plate 67) the two who are holding hands have forgotten that it would show in the picture! The girl involved, Carrie Clark, is only seventeen here. She had a glorious voice and became a noted singer, but her too ample proportions kept her from achieving the opera. (During the First World War she sang for the soldiers all over Europe.)

Another flashlight (Plate 70), a very poor picture, is included here only because it shows another of the popular diversions of the eighties. The Dakins and their group played planchette or, as it was sometimes called, the ouija board, by the hour. One of their guests, Jessie Messmore, was considered very psychic and when her fingers touched the board something always began to happen. It would even answer her questions in French, although she knew not a word of that language herself! One day, when Mrs. Judge Campbell asked planchette where her jewelry was that had disappeared, it answered, "Under the bed in the servants' room," and sure enough there she found it.

66. Music at "Uplawn": (at left) Floy Dakin and Letitia Hart: (at piano) Anna Maria Dakin and Harvey Loomis: (standing in rear) Leonard. Carrie Clark, Paul: (by lamp) Alice White

67. Interior flash at "Uplawn": (l. to r.) a boy holding Carrie Clark's hand, Maria Campbell, Floy Dakin, Ella Herrick, Will Campbell, Frank Herrick, Hallie Campbell, Jessie Messmore Dakin, Douglas Campbell (on floor, front), Harvey Loomis

68. Early experiment with flashlight in "Uplawn" library: Anna Maria Dakin (left), Jessie Messmore Dakin (center), George Dakin (right)

Amateur dramatics and charades were extremely popular, and the Dakin boys had a hand printing press with which they printed quite professional-looking programs for their plays. George Dakin, an excellent actor, often took the leading male role and directed the plays. *The Happiest Day of My Life* was so successful that they gave it several times for the public at Union Hall. Other plays that were a great success were *Box and Cox* or, *The Long Lost Brothers,* a comic opera in one act from the book by F. C. Burmond, with music by Arthur S. Sullivan, and *Il Jacoby.* The latter had come out as an operetta, using the current popular songs that everyone knew.

The charade photograph (Plate 73), obviously representing the word "faint," shows the traditional pose for a group gathered around a fainting figure and charming solicitude in the face of the girl who is chafing the hand of the victim. That is Anna Miles Olcott, and the girl with the bottle of smelling salts is Floy Dakin, who were both at Hollins Institute in the winter. A set of their tableaux called "Living Pictures" showed, in one picture, a dentist at work on a patient's teeth. The others had to guess the title, which proved in this case to be, "Excavation of Ancient Ruins!"

There were other diversions, too, of course, of which there are no photographs—all sorts of guessing and writing games such as crambo and dumb crambo at their evening gatherings. There were also Welsh rabbit parties and overnight visiting from house to house, which the young people today would call pajama parties.

But the most popular indoor diversion was dancing, now that the more intimate round dances were taking the place of the old-time

69. Interior flash: George Dakin (standing, right) telling a funny story in "Uplawn" library to his daughter (standing beside him), his wife (at table, left), daughter-in-law (at table, right), Mary Marvin Olcott, a cousin of Grandfather Olcott (left), and others

70. September 14, 1888. Flash: Planchette at "Uplawn," Jessie and Leonard at center table

71. July 16, 1886. "Three Little Maids from School": Harriet Olcott, Annie Wright, Floy Dakin

square dances. An early *Harper's* article protested that no pure woman would suffer a man to retain her hand in his, much less strain her to his breast publicly for a quarter of an hour at a time. The etiquette manuals accepted the new round dances with some caution, warning: In waltzing "a gentleman never encircles the lady's waist until the dance begins, and drops his arms as soon as it ends." Then the attitude developed that "there is impropriety in the suggestion of impropriety."*

In the late eighties the two-step swung gaily into fashion with John Philip Sousa's colorful marches and became quite as popular as the slower waltzes. Both Leonard Dakin and his mother needed to hear these tunes only once to be able to play them off by ear. (Years later Anna Maria nearly convulsed her grandchildren in church one Sunday when she, as organist, improvised for the prelude a colorful but dignified composition, played slowly and in a minor key, based on "Alexander's Ragtime Band," which she had been playing for them to dance a romping two-step to the evening before.)

In Cherry Valley many families had at least one formal ball each summer climaxed with a cotillion, which was the most fashionable dance in the eighties. At "Woodbine," when they danced informally it was on the nailed-down carpet, but for these formal balls a canvas was stretched over the carpet. One of the gayest social events of the season was the big German, complete with favors, given by the Park House Hotel next to "Woodbine."

*Quoted in ARTHUR M. SCHLESINGER, *Learning How to Behave* (New York: Macmillan, 1947), pp. 44-45.

72. Leonard (right), Paul (next), and friends burlesque the "Three Little Maids" and Poo-Bah from *The Mikado*

One summer two of the young men guests gave a long-remembered party at the Park House, a costume ball to which all came dressed as little children. One of the prizes went to the thin young man in the derby hat seen sitting on the ground at the extreme right in Plate 93. This youth was not very popular with the girls, who thought he looked as if he had been buried and dug up again. He appeared at the ball in one of their small brother's suits with Little Lord Fauntleroy collar and cuffs.

It was after one of the formal dances at "Woodbine" that one of the guests saw a picture she could never forget. Accustomed to the quaint formalities of connubial restraint, she probably had never heard Mr. Olcott call Mrs. Olcott anything so intimate even as "dear." But this evening when she ran back to pick up a scarf she had forgotten, there at the foot of the stairs was Mr. Olcott putting his arms about his wife and drawing her toward him. "Yes, Hat," he was saying as he smoothed her hair back from her brow and gently kissed her, "I know you are tired, but what a charming hostess you are and what a beautiful time you gave all your guests!" "If you think that, Mr. Olcott, then I don't care how tired I am." And for a moment she put her head down on his shoulder. The young guest, holding her breath, tip-toed quietly away.

73. July 21, 1888. Charades: (l. to r.) Floy Dakin, Grace Olmstead, Jessie
Messmore, Anna Miles Olcott (Nannie)

Leonard Stops Action

BOTH the front piazza and the south porch at "Uplawn" were in daily use, opening by French windows from the parlor and library, and the parlor was in more common use than in most homes before that sanctum of decorum was made over into the modern living room.

The photograph (Plate 75) on and around the front piazza bears witness to what Edward Steichen has described as Leonard's "sensitive, pictorial sense." Here one observes bustled figures in picture hats at each far side facing in, and the ease and grace of the smaller groups within the whole. The stately figure in black in the right foreground is only seventeen years old. This was her first dress with a bustle, and although the front of the dress was beautifully embroidered with gold braid, she begged Leonard for this pose with her back to the camera because she thought her rear view so ravishing!

For these Cherry Valley youths, most diversion on these happy summer days took place out-of-doors. Here (Plate 76) in playful mood is a group of young people romping on the lawn. The boy who is pushing a girl in a wheelbarrow looks as if he were running an obstacle race.

The view of the lawn in Plate 77 shows the new game of lawn tennis, which had been introduced into this country from England (via Bermuda) about a decade before. The original hour-glass-

74. On the front piazza at "Uplawn": the Rev. Henry U. Swinnerton on steps, Leonard in white next to him, Jessie hatless and pouting (center), family and friends

75. August 9, 1887. "Uplawn": (l. to r., on ground) Maud Perry, Howard
Campbell, Mrs. Howard Campbell (Jessie's sister Lizzie), Ned Dix, Alice
White, Miss Pegrim; (on piazza) Anna Maria Dakin, Will Campbell, Emma
Olcott, Mary Campbell, Mary White, Joe White, Floy Dakin, Sutherland Reed
Haxston, Eloise Bennett, Miss Johnson, Frances Pierson, Marion Olcott, Grace O.
Campbell, May Leonard, another guest, Will Dix; (standing in front) Carrie
Clark, Walter Campbell, Hallie Campbell, Jessie Messmore; (seated in front)
Harriet Olcott, Harvey Loomis

shaped court had long since yielded to the present conventional shape by the time the game reached Cherry Valley, where the Dakins had one of the first sets in the village. The girl standing by a canvas sunshade (that was stretched over a red cane settee) is holding a man's long bow for archery, the target for which is across the lawn at the left.

In the summer of 1886 Leonard became keenly interested in taking photographs of people in action. The game of tennis as played by beginners offered opportunity for his first experiments in this field.

In the first doubles picture (Plate 78) there is more interest in the rear view of the girl's tennis costume than in the action! In the second doubles picture (Plate 79) it is obvious that the shutter is not fast enough to catch the ball, seen at the left over the net as a blur. And although there is action, it is of a rather deliberate sort, which did not satisfy Leonard.

In the photograph of a singles match (Plate 80) there is definite action on the part of the man in the foreground, whose racket is moving so fast as to be almost invisible, but the whole negative was too thin. The negligent, casual-looking player on the far side of the net looks as if she has absolutely no expectation of the ball's being returned to her.

Not only was the action in these tennis pictures too deliberate for the young photographer, but only one person in them was in action at once. So imagine his delight when he thought up a new sport one day—jumping over the tennis net! Here was real action. That was what he wanted. But he found that his shutter was not fast enough

76. August 14, 1888. Teenagers romping on the lawn

77. A summer afternoon at "Uplawn"

78. Tennis at "Uplawn": Paul Dakin (behind umbrella) on far side of net

79. Tennis at "Uplawn": (l. to r.) Paul Dakin, Hallie Campbell, Will Campbell, Mr. Stonyson (a guest of the Campbells)

80. Man in action at "Uplawn." Experiment with homemade speed shutter

and his first action pictures were not very good. For example, the figures in the first jumping one (Plate 81) are all blurred.

The lens in Leonard's camera was not corrected to cover the entire exposure evenly and the center of the picture was clearer than the outer parts. He could overcome this in taking a still group by posing the people in a curve that corresponded to the curve of the lens. But there was no curve to a tennis net!

Gradually Leonard improved his technique, but he had to use some ingenuity to produce such successful pictures even as these. His camera was of the old-fashioned single lens bellows type with a plate-holder attachment and a wooden shutter that was released by a lever and fell by gravity. He finally succeeded in speeding this up by the use of elastic bands and by controlling the timing until he got pictures that are comparable to the high-speed camera shot of today.

In Plate 89, except for a light streak through a chip in the plate holder, we have a clear, sharp photograph of rapid action close to the camera, together with a depth of focus that shows the house in the background only slightly blurred.

An elderly photographer who had worked with the old plate-holder type of camera back in the eighties and nineties marvelled at the patience which these two photographs (Plates 90 and 91) represent in Leonard Dakin's work. To make one picture look as if a group were taking off for a standing broad jump and another to look as if the group were coming down from such a jump must have involved considerable planning, readying of the camera, the focus, and the plates; but Leonard was a perfectionist, careful in everything

81. Blurred attempt to stop action

82. August 14, 1888. A close-up of three leapers. Success in stopping action

83. September 4, 1888. Leaping over tennis net

84. September 4, 1888. Some of Dakin's early action shots were thin

85. September 4, 1888. Jumping over net: (l. to r.) Paul Dakin, Marion
Olcott, Mary Campbell, Horace Olcott, Maud Perry, Jessie Messmore, Leonard
Dakin, a guest, Floy Dakin, Harriet Olcott, Horatio L. Olcott

86. September 4, 1888. Fun for the photographer

87. September 4, 1888. A flurry of legs and petticoats

88. September 4, 1888. Slow in getting started

89. August 20, 1888. Sam Campbell, Paul Dakin, and Walter Campbell leaping high

he did and never in a hurry. Perhaps one should think also of the patience of his subjects who did so much jumping for him in their tight, hot clothes; but, except for the girl in white who is having difficulty with her hat, they all look as if they were enjoying it.

In Plate 92 the three figures at the right seem suspended in mid-air. A writer for the Hartford *Courant* (October 18, 1951) asked when viewing this picture, "Who is that Nijinsky, three in from the right, headed for the stratosphere? Better retract that landing gear, Space Boy!" These two groups on the lawn (Plates 93 and 94) might be compositions by an impressionist painter. The chiaroscuro as the sunlight plays in pattern through the leaves gives the photograph this delightful effect. Such a composition is not accidental. Leonard Dakin had the consummate eye of an artist and a sensitive feeling for pictorial design.

The group effectively posed about a table on the lawn (Plate 95) shows Leonard Dakin himself seated on the ground. He has arranged the composition, focused the camera, slipped the black cover from the face of the plate in readiness, and taken his position in the foreground. Leonard took all the still pictures that he is in himself by running a thread from the camera to where he sat. But here one might guess that he is anxiously watching a friend whom he has asked to make the exposure for him. No one else in the photograph is looking at the camera or seems at all concerned about the result. In the few jumping pictures where he himself is jumping he probably had his brother Paul take the picture for him.

In the charming composition (Plate 96), with the long line of

90. August 23, 1888. Broad jump at "Uplawn": (l. to r.) half of Nannie
Olcott, Jessie Messmore, Marion Olcott, Mary Campbell, Sam Campbell, Maud
Perry, Paul Dakin

91. August 23, 1888. Happy landing! (l. to r.) Paul Dakin, Mary Campbell, Nannie Olcott, Sammy Campbell, Jessie Messmore, Marion Dix, Maud Perry

92. August 20, 1888. Jumping over net

93. September 1, 1887. An impressionistic photograph: (standing) Will Dix, Ned Dix, Will Campbell; (back row, seated) Marion Olcott, Maria Campbell, Letitia Hart, Floy Dakin, Miss Johnson; (front row, seated) Emma Olcott, a guest, Howard Browning, Grace Olmstead, Paul Dakin, Jessie Messmore, Hallie Campbell, Joe White, Mary Campbell, Grace McCloud, S. R. Haxston; (lying in front) Larry Olmstead

94. Like a sun-dappled Renoir painting: (back row) Grace Campbell, Paul
Dakin, Jessie Messmore, a guest, Hallie Campbell, Floy Dakin, Maria Campbell,
a guest, Marion Olcott: (on ground, front) Walter Campbell, Grace Olmstead,
Howard Browning (feet on fur rug)

the old-fashioned string hammock cutting diagonally across it, the height of the figures gradually ascends from each side toward the center, forming a low pyramid. The only boy in this group of pretty girls is Paul, who wears his full beard boldly. He is about twenty-five in most of these pictures, recently home from Hamilton College where beards were "in."

Beards had been "in," of course, since the Civil War, Grover Cleveland in 1885 being our first clean-shaven President since that conflict. But beards were on the way out now. In the late eighties Lydia E. White's *Success in Society* stated that "beards have gone out of fashion. No one should wear a beard unless he have a pre-ternaturally ugly mouth and chin."* In Plates 60, 61, 66, 93, and 107 Paul's beard has been reduced to sideburns. But his white-vested friend, Larry Olmsted, still clings to his full beard in spite of the changing style.

Beards were not the only style subject to the changing times. In these photographs no men are seen smoking, for they did not often smoke in the presence of ladies. However, the attitude of women toward this Victorian dictum was changing. Whereas an earlier manual laid down the law: "Never smoke in ladies' presence even on the street," one published in 1887 stated that "ladies no longer affect to be disgusted by the odor of tobacco," and another regarded a cigar (though not a pipe) as allowable "when by the seaside or in the country . . . if your fair companion does not object." But one,

*Quoted in ARTHUR M. SCHLESINGER, *Learning How to Behave* (New York: Macmillan, 1947), p. 38.

95. August 30, 1887. Group by fence at "Uplawn": (back row, l. to r.) Daisy
Vanderlip (seated), Anna Maria Dakin, Carrie Clark, Floy Dakin, Harvey
Loomis, Frank Bainbridge, Grace O. Borst (seated), May Vanderlip, Larry
Olmstead; (seated, front) Leonard and Paul Dakin

even as late as 1891, with ominous foreboding declared: "We think the prospects for the future happiness of that young girl are small, who will be seen in public with a gentleman who is smoking."*

*Ibid., p. 39.

96. August 8, 1890. Relaxing after a game of tennis: (l. to r.) Maria Campbell, May Leonard, Eloise Bennett (in hammock), Harriet Leonard, Harriet Olcott, Frances Pierson (behind H.O.), Elise Phillips, Jessie Dakin holding her baby Roland; (on ground) Floy Dakin, Ruth Greenleaf, Nannie Olcott, Paul Dakin

Bustles and Bowlers

IT IS HARD TO BELIEVE that practically all the people in these photographs are girls in their teens and boys in their twenties. (See, e.g., Plate 96.) The plump figure looking down in the upper center, Frances Pierson, is only nineteen here. She looks much older in a black gown in Plate 120, sitting on the south porch steps. She used to say that when she reached forty she intended to wear a cap. Needless to say, when that time arrived she had changed her mind. In Plate 96 the pretty girl in the hammock in a dark suit, Eloise Bennett, Floy's roommate from Hollins, is only eighteen. In this group of tennis players (Plate 97) the youth at the right, Edwin Asa Dix, who is older (twenty-seven), has recently been on a trip abroad, and now wears a Roman sash and a French beret.

Groups of young people you do not know, standing around in modern dress, would ordinarily be dull to look at. Even girls and boys jumping over a tennis net in shorts today would not be very thrilling. But in the costume of the eighties, especially with their bustles, it is different! The fact that they would jump over a net in such costumes proves that they were young; no middle-aged person would dare take the risk. Indeed, these are what our modern youth would call the teenagers, the bobby-soxers of their time!

They were as much interested in style then as the young people are today. And the style of the eighties dictated, as Plate 99 well illustrates, that the emphasis in women's clothes should be on the skirt. Skirts were narrow and straight or draped in front with most of the fullness toward the back, where the bustle was large, although not so large as it had been in the seventies. They were gathered, plaited, or elaborately draped, which gave opportunity for great elegance even in simple materials and plain patterns. The skirts of the eighties just cleared the ground. By 1892 the walking costume had its train. But only evening gowns now or the full-dressed toilet, as it was called, had long trains, and these were elaborately trimmed with embroidery, ruching, fringes, lace, and bows.

Dresses were often made of different materials in the same color or in contrasting colors, charming effects being obtained where several shades of the same color were tastefully blended. Black silk was in especially good taste. Every married woman, no matter how limited her wardrobe, possessed one black watered silk, often trimmed with large jet buttons, for Sunday best.

While the fashion interest through the eighties concentrated on the skirt, the bodice received scant attention. At the close of the seventies the fashion for closeness of fit had reached a pitch beyond which it was impossible to go. In Plate 100, which shows a row of girls on the fence, we see the long, tight-fitting bodice, often ending in a point. The wasp-waist of the thirties and forties had yielded to an average waist of seventeen or eighteen inches in the sixties, when it was thought that if lacing were begun early enough it was not injurious. The *Century Magazine* of October, 1915, tells us that

97. Tennis costumes in the eighties

"the supple and growing frame of a young girl will accommodate itself to any form or direction with perfect ease." But even now, in the eighties, it was said that in smart society, the smaller they made their waists by lacing, the more many women truly thought they were of aristocratic stock. Perhaps the girls in these pictures wore the "Pivot Corset," an 1884 advertisement for which ran: "It expands and contracts with the breathing, and yields to every movement of the wearer, making an Easy and Elegant fit. $1.00."

As these pictures show, bosoms and hips must be rounded, and arms as tightly covered as possible. If Nature had not endowed a woman with a bosom of stylish proportions, she wore finely gathered ruffles, one over the other, sewn onto a foundation that could be pinned across the corset cover. One guest at "Uplawn" was long remembered as "flat-chested Fanny." No one would ever have known about her natural deficiency, however, had she not so delighted in producing horrified squeals by sticking her hat pins, whenever she took off her hat, into her bosom as one might into pincushions.

Floy's cousin tells the tale that when Annie thought Floy was too young to wear these deceptive ruffles, Leonard complained one day that his socks were gradually disappearing. Then the truth came out. By stuffing one more pair of socks in her dress every few days Floy had thought she could appear to be developing naturally a well-rounded figure!

In general there were no sports clothes for the girl of the eighties except the riding habit. Sidesaddle was the only conceivable way of riding, and a long one-sided skirt trailed down below the foot that

98. August 14, 1888. Bustles in action

was in the stirrup. A Butterick Pattern for a Ladies' Riding-habit in 1887 says: "Skirt is shaped to be graceful and comfortable whether the wearer be mounted or walking. The basque is finely shaped and adjusted by the fashionable number of gracefully curved seams and darts. . . . The trousers . . . are usually made of the same material. . . . Above the knees, however, they may be made of chamois if preferred." There was to be a pocket in the skirt. Such a medium-sized habit would require 5 ⅜ yards of material 54 inches wide. A stove-pipe hat was worn with this habit.

When lawn tennis first emerged as the favorite sport, it was called "an elegant and pleasant pastime," and was considered a "proper activity for young ladies," although no lady would think of serving overhand. From the "Fashion Notes" in *Arthur's Home Magazine*, published in Philadelphia during the eighties, we learn of the earliest tennis outfits for women. The contrast to our simple tennis costumes of today is so marked that it is worth quoting in full.

There are already many charming patterns of lawn-tennis gowns, shown in soft, wool materials and delicate shades of crêpe de chine, they are draped so as not to seem to divide into upper and lower skirts, and front breadths, but to show no edges as though it were tacked round the hem, turned upward, and then caught down here and there where the folds fall naturally. The soft striped flannels for tennis are most comfortably made, with blouse waists, kilted skirts, and apron drapery. The kilt has no foundation skirt, so that it may be very light, its plaits being

99. August 9, 1887. Dress parade

held by two or three sets of tapes. The short apron has the stripes taken crosswise, and in the back is the butterfly drapery made of two breadths caught up high in the middle and made to form two points like wings. The blouse is like the sailor blouse worn by children, with a runner in the hem, and drooping below the waist. A straight band is set down the front between two plaits, sewn on one side and buttoned under the plait opposite. The sleeves are full, gathered into a straight cuff, a high, narrow, turned-over collar, and a deep, wide collar, broad and square-cornered behind, with the fronts ending in points, and pushed through a strap like a sailor-knotted scarf. An outside jacket to be worn with this has loose fronts fastened only at the throat, tight fitting back, square side pockets, turned-over collar.

But there were no such costumes as this in Cherry Valley, for here they played in the same dresses that they wore all the time.

And they did wear the same dresses all the time. The same ones appear again and again in these photographs. For here they were certainly nearer the extreme of two hundred years earlier when, it is said, the styles changed so slowly that a woman sometimes wore the same dress for the greater part of her life, than they were to the opposite extreme of the smart set of their day, who vacationed at the fashionable hotels in Saratoga Springs. There no elegant lady ever wore the same gown twice and consequently she had to have so many gowns that the Saratoga trunk was invented to carry them.

100. September 1, 1887. Tight bodices for the girls, a variety of hats for the boys: (on fence, l. to r.) Jessie Messmore, Mary Campbell, Floy Dakin, Letitia Hart, Maria Campbell, Miss Johnson, Miss Van Vrankin, Emma Olcott, a guest, Hallie Campbell, Joe White, Marion Olcott, Grace McCloud; (on ground) Larry Olmstead, Ned Dix, S. R. Haxston, Will Dix, Will Campbell, Howard Browning

No wonder *Godey's Lady's Book* called Saratoga and Newport "the Sodom and Gomorrah of our Union!"

When these girls dressed in the morning, if the day promised to be warm, they might put on a light dress of dotted or figured muslin; on a cool day they wore cashmere dresses trimmed with braid or a heavier wool, for ladies of refinement did not wear sweaters in those days. And they dressed once for the whole day unless there were going to be a formal party in the evening.

Consider what they had to put on and compare it with what a modern girl wears. First, two undergarments (never omitted); corsets, tight-laced; a corset-cover which was often high-necked to protect the gown from soilure; a knee-length petticoat of flannel except on the hottest days when it was of muslin; at least two long petticoats over which a bustle was tied in the rear; and then a dress that reached from chin to ankle. Long black or brown stockings of cotton or fine cashmere wool and high shoes were part of the outfit, too. Gloves and shoes both fitted snugly, for hands and feet must look small. Black patent leather shoes with cloth tops were ultra-fashionable, laced or in the newer buttoned style.

If there is any doubt as to what garment was worn under the short petticoat, here is the answer (Plate 101)! But most of the jumping girls show at least the ruffles on their long petticoats. When Jessie Messmore made a petticoat for Marion Olcott's trousseau, it had so many rows of lace insertion and edging that the bridegroom calculated the length of stitching by the measure of the bridge over the Marrisquam River where he took Marion sailing.

101. O-oh!

Such exposures as these pictures produced were shocking beyond our conception today. The appearance of an ankle was so rare as to be material for a novelist's comment. And ministers of that day were known to preach against the popular but wicked game of croquet because it offered a girl an opportunity to lift her skirt a few inches while sending her opponent's ball. As a matter of fact, if Leonard Dakin had ever shown these pictures to the people in them, they would never have jumped before his camera again. He *did not* show them!

You will notice that in Plates 103 and 104 one of the ladies seems to be holding back. That is Jessie Messmore to whom Leonard Dakin was in the process of becoming engaged this summer. She is the one in black, which she is wearing because she is in mourning for her nineteen-year-old sister who has recently died of consumption. Here she is wearing Leonard's striped sports cap, and she is holding back because she alone was admitted to the darkroom with him and knew the terrible truth of what these pictures revealed. Together they went into gales of laughter as each new picture was developed, but they never told. She knew that there were no legs in the Victorian cult of decency, that for a girl even to cross her legs in company marked her as "common." Observe, therefore, how decorously she jumps and compare her with the girl at the left whose hat is cocked over one eye and whose "limbs" are exposed all the way to the knee.

In Plate 105 the girl standing at the upper left has a neckline almost down to her collarbone. The fashion was for high necks,

102. August 20, 1888. Gracefully soaring

103. August 20, 1888. Jessie, wearing Leonard's cap, jumps decorously

104. Defying the Victorian cult of decency, which forbade cocked hats and exposed limbs

many of the dresses having boned net attachable collars. But this young fifteen-year-old took the game of tennis very seriously and tired of playing tennis in a stiff, high-collared shirtwaist and long, stiff skirt. She *had* to play in corsets, for an uncorseted woman was a bawdy woman then; but, having a natural flair for dressmaking and some imagination, she made this daring new "low-necked" sport dress for tennis herself, without any pattern. When she returned to boarding school that fall the girls were so crazy about it that they all copied it for their sportswear. This lady played tennis until long after she was a grandmother, and she always served underhand. As a girl she used to come home from parties at Hyde Hall on Otsego Lake and make drawings of the pretty dresses worn by a very smartly dressed girl from New York who visited there and, with the help of a dressmaker, copy them for herself.

Butterick patterns were in general use at this time and many families had a seamstress in the house who could use them, as well as an outside dressmaker, for there were no ready-made clothes then as now. Mrs. Slater, the seamstress at "Woodbine," who often had headaches, had to have her coffee with lemon in it before she could begin to sew. To be a seamstress took real wit. With our easy patterns of today, we would be aghast at the number of pieces of those earlier ones and unequal to the complicated directions. Foot-run sewing machines were just replacing the awkward hand-crank ones that came into use after the Civil War, but much of the work was still done by hand. Of course there were no dry cleaners in those days, and in order to wash many of the more elaborately made dresses, one had

105. Summer hats were large in the eighties

to take them apart and make them up again after the pieces were washed. They used what was known as soap-tree bark for washing them. Kid gloves were cleaned by suspending them from the stopper of a tall glass jar in the bottom of which was strong ammonia and, after leaving them there for a day, rubbing them with bread crumbs.

Godey's Lady's Book, the edifying and genteel feminine magazine and fashion guide, had lost much of its vitality by the eighties, but Cherry Valley was fortunate in having two expert dressmakers, Mrs. VanDyke and Josephine Reynolds. The latter always sat cross-legged on a table while she sewed, like a tailor. She had two sisters of renown. Annie, a pampered butterfly, was given to loud-voiced prayer with windows and doors wide open when she wanted financial assistance—a roof reshingled or even a bottle of whiskey for emergencies—and Grandmother Olcott seemed to be her general victim and benefactor. Her other sister, Mary, was the expert buttonhole maker, assistant to Josephine, and together they produced creations equal to the styles in *Vogue* today. Indeed, such smart gowns could Josephine Reynolds turn out that when the Borse family fell upon hard times and decided to send their beautiful, delicate Sophie to New York to try to catch a wealthy husband, they staked their all on an elegant outfit made by Josephine. Sophie won her man and what matter that he had eleven children to boot!

Annie Reynolds was one of those Cherry Valley characters whose sayings have lived after them. When Grandfather Olcott, complimenting her on her appearance one day, said, "How well you are looking, Miss Reynolds," she replied, "Vicey vercey to you, Mr.

106. July 26, 1888. Only a little old lady's bonnet for Ella (extreme left), already in her forties

Olcott." And on his seventy-ninth birthday she remarked, "Why Mr. Olcott, you will soon be an octogeranium!"

Hats were usually large in the eighties, profusely decorated with flowers and plumes. In the "Fashion Notes" in *Arthur's Home Magazine* for October, 1887, we read, "Dyed wings and whole birds, sad to say, will be used more than ever." A girl would almost as soon go out of doors without a dress as without a hat. If by chance she has no hat she will always have a parasol to protect her complexion. And sometimes, we observe, she even has both. The "Fashion Notes" advised, "Parasols are plainer this season than last, but they must always match the dress and the bonnet." Not so in Cherry Valley, evidently.

In Plate 107 there are five closed parasols besides the three open ones. The girl under the second one from the right is Jessie Messmore at the age of twenty, two years before she married Leonard Dakin. He carried this little picture of her in a gold locket on his watch chain for over fifty years.

In Plate 106 the figure seated on the ground at the extreme left is Ella Olcott, young Horatio's wife, who has recently passed her fortieth birthday. No big picture hat for her anymore, but a modest little old lady's bonnet that ties under the chin! Several of the girls at the right have taken their hats off, and little Julie in the center, aged four, has on enough hat for two.

Men's hats were picturesque, too. The hurdling picture (Plate 108) is a good study in men's hats: the bowler and the sports cap. Of course top hats were worn much more informally in the eighties

107. Umbrellas to protect the complexion: (on fence, l. to r.) Mary Harriott, Emma Olcott, Mary Campbell, Paul Dakin, Hallie Campbell, Floy Dakin, Jessie Messmore, Grace Campbell, Julia Little; (seated on bench) May Leonard (feathers on hat), Frances Pierson, Joe White, Harriet Olcott; (on ground) Carrie Clark, S. R. Haxston, Letitia Hart, Harvey Loomis, Alice White

than they are today, sometimes even in sports. (See, e.g., the sailing picture, Plate 60.)

Sports clothes for men seem to have made a start at this time. Many of the boys in these photographs are wearing gaily striped blazers with caps to match. But even these are often buttoned high to the neck. The shirts, usually stiffly starched throughout, had detachable cuffs and collars of the wing type, though occasionally soft collars were worn for sports. Also "linene, reversible, button-on collars and cuffs for men" are mentioned in "Fashion Notes" for May, 1887. The coats were generally double-breasted, interlined, and padded; trousers were tight and, as Allan Nevins tells us, "men regarded trouser creases, a sign of the store shelf, with distaste."* Leonard Dakin continued to have his suits made to order at Brooks Brothers, but Paul began about this time to buy ready-made suits at Brokaw Brothers, and then would have the creases pressed out of the trousers before he wore them. (This reminds one that the ladies let their maids wear their gloves until the new was off them.) Gold watch chains were looped across the men's vests, which were never removed for even the most violent exercise. To appear in shirt sleeves was considered so common that the boys in Plate 109 would never have done so had any ladies been present.

The frock coat, which was rapidly losing favor now, appears in only two of these photographs. It had once been considered the only proper attire for a man in a lady's parlor.

*A History of American Life (New York: Macmillan, 1927), p. 210.

194

108. August 14, 1888. Leonard, Paul, and Walter Campbell leap over tennis net to the delight of the ladies

Up to the early eighties the men had worn boots nearly knee-high inside their trousers. They were made to order by a local cobbler. A cobbler's advertisement in an old issue of the *Cherry Valley Gazette* was remarkably polite, stating:

> The subscriber informs his customers and the public in general that he continues the business of *Boot and Shoe Making.* . . . The subscriber tenders his grateful acknowledgments to the public for the liberal patronage which he has received, and hopes by unremitted attention to his business, to merit a continuance of it.

Many of the advertisements of this period read: "Most kinds of produce received for work." At the time of these photographs high-laced shoes for men were replacing boots, but they were still, for the most part, being made to order by the cobbler.

When the men jump over a rope it is high and taut; when the girls jump, the men swing the rope for them. When some of these photographs appeared in the February 9, 1948, issue of *Life,* that magazine remarked of Plate 110, "A girl can still be ladylike while jumping rope if she wears veil and gloves." We have called this an age of complacency. Could any creature look more complacent, more utterly pleased with herself than the veiled and gloved girl in the second rope-jumping picture? She is eighteen; the girl at the left is only fifteen; the one at the right is seventeen.

The one at the right is Marion Olcott, who later recalled: "Until I was fourteen years of age my interests were altogether those of a

109. Perry Olcott, Leonard Dakin, Walter Campbell, and Paul Dakin jump
a tight rope

110. August 23, 1888. Sam Campbell (left) and Paul Dakin (right) turn rope for Mary Campbell (fifteen), Maud Perry (eighteen), and Marion Olcott (seventeen)

111. August 23, 1888. "Salt, ginger, mustard." Maud Perry (center) can be ladylike skipping rope if she wears veil and gloves

child; then I seemed suddenly to grow into young ladyhood."
Perhaps to her at fourteen a "young lady" was characterized by what
she wore rather than by what she did. Consider these "young ladies"
climbing over fences and jumping off them! It is true that our general
impression of the young people of the seventies and the eighties is that
maturity came to them earlier than to the young people of today.
Doubtless we are led to that impression not only by the older-looking
clothes they wore at so early an age, but by the stiffly posed photographs we usually see of them. Leonard Dakin's pictures, however,
prove the contrary to be true.

Maturity of demeanor came with matrimony. When the young
people married they took their homemaking and parental responsi-
bilities very seriously, usually giving up the activities of youth, and
were seldom seen in the rollicking adventures that had characterized
their single days. But not so the Dakin children's aunt, Grace Olcott
Campbell. She is seen here in picture after picture leaping over the
net with her nieces and nephews, a little slower in getting started
perhaps, but always there. In the photograph showing the girls
climbing over a rail fence (Plate 112), she is the one at the right
still gathering up her skirts to make the climb while others are halfway over; and in the photograph showing them leaping off the fence
(Plate 113), she is the one hesitating on the fence top when the
others are already in the air. But although she was only eight years
older than her eldest nephew, she was middle-aged now, that is,
she had passed into her thirties, and one must admire her zest for
living, her determination to stay young.

Even in such clothes the girls could manage a fence without too much difficulty, especially if Paul Dakin stood on the farther side to urge them on. But one wonders how they ever managed to climb a tree as they once did when on a walk through a pasture they were chased by a bull!

The bustles show up better perhaps in these rope-jumping and fence-climbing pictures than in any of the others, and of course the pictures would not be half so amusing without them. A contemporary advertisement for bustles read: "Light, cool and comfortable. Recommended by fashionable ladies. Always regains shape after pressure." When a certain young cousin came to live with the George Dakins, she was so thin that Grandfather Olcott said to his wife, "Hat, can't you put a bustle on that girl?"

These photographs were taken in 1886. By '88 bustles began to diminish; they were scarcely noticeable by '89, and had vanished entirely by 1890.

112. August 14, 1888. Climbing the fence: (l. to r.) Mary Campbell, Nannie Olcott, Emma Olcott, Jessie Messmore, a friend, Mary Harriott, Grace Campbell

113. August 14, 1888. Grace Campbell, the middle-aged jumper, hesitates to make the plunge

114. August 14, 1888. Paul urges girls to hurry up as they climb fence

115. High-buttoned coats and creaseless trousers at "Uplawn"

Sports and Diversions

ONE must not get the impression that tennis was the only game these young people played or that "Uplawn" was the only place where they gathered. The jolly times at "Uplawn" and "Woodbine" are typical of happy days in other homes in Cherry Valley. We tell the story of this particular group simply because their story happens to have photographs to illustrate it. In addition to facilities at "Uplawn," there was a tennis court at "Auchinbreck," the Campbell place up on the hill, where the group often met, but we have only one picture that Leonard took of a gathering there (Plate 116).

Archery was very popular, with a target at both "Uplawn" and "Woodbine." There was an Archery Club, and each person had his own bow and arrows. In Plate 117 one can see the smaller size of the girls' bow and quiver. The young man at the left in the top hat, a Presbyterian minister, seems a bit unhappy as he looks resolutely out of the picture. One wonders why he ever let himself get into such a crowded position there among the ladies!

Far behind the garden at "Woodbine" the Dakins and their group practiced pistol shooting at a mark or at empty beer bottles. The young people did not go on long hikes in the eighties as they often do today. Once several of them tried it, walking six miles to the neighboring town of Sharon Springs and six miles back. This proved too ambitious an undertaking, especially for the girls in all their warm, tight clothing. Everyone got tired out and disgusted with the venture, which was not repeated.

It was far greater fun and less fatiguing, when the circus came to town, to sit under the big tent and eat popcorn and peanuts or feed them to the elephants. Even as P. T. Barnum's "Great Moral Show" laid strong emphasis on the elevating character of his circus, so the lesser circuses that came to Cherry Valley sometimes had Biblical scenes painted on the sides of the animal wagons and gave free passes to clergymen and editors. Although Barnum was traveling by railroad in the early seventies instead of in wagons, it was not until June 11, 1889, that the first railroad circus reached Cherry Valley. It consisted of eleven cars. Levere Winne discovered an old ledger which reveals that the twenty-one principals of this Walter L. Main's Show, including "Colorado Joe," "Wild Bear," and "Madame Du Bois," stayed at the Winne House, the hotel nearest the railroad. They were called at 4:45 A.M., breakfasted at 5, dined at 11, and had supper at 5:30, putting on an afternoon and an evening performance of their circus. There was always a holiday atmosphere in the air so long as the circus was in town. The streets were crowded with farmers' families in from the country, and vendors selling candy, balloons, and sparkling pinchbeck jewelry took all the children's spending money.

When the excitement of the circus was over, the young people might return to an unfinished battle of croquet. For their croquet matches were a continuing affair that went on and on. If it grew dark

208

116. July 25, 1888. Group at "Auchinbreck," home of the Campbell family

before a desperate and decisive contest was completed, they sometimes played by lantern light or even put candles on the wickets.

At "Woodbine" the croquet lawn was separated by the syringa hedge from the church lawn where money-raising fairs were often held. At one of these fairs Mrs. Stringer, when she was one hundred years old, demonstrated her skill in spinning flax into thread, which was sold at a cent a yard for the benefit of the church. But the children were more interested in the monthly church suppers, luscious ten-cent feasts that would interrupt any croquet game.

At these church suppers the younger people usually tried to take a piece of each kind of cake that was passed. It was amazing what a record some of them could make, but often it was physically impossible to do away with all that one had heaped upon his plate in happy anticipation. However, these untouched pieces were far from wasted.

For there subsisted across the street from these church suppers Mrs. Margaret Woodburn, personification of respectable gentility. She was a widow who lived behind a picket fence in a closely shuttered house with her thrall Fanny (called "Tarzy" by the boys) and her twenty-five cats. The brick building in which her father, Amasa Belknap, the famed gunsmith, had had his shop stood in the yard close by. How her husband, Dr. Woodburn, who was a fine physician, squandered or lost his money no one knows. It is enough that he died young and left his widow an income of sixty dollars a year. Out of this, over the years, with pride she saved up three hundred dollars for her funeral expenses.

117. August 10, 1888. Archery was a favorite sport: (standing at l.) Grace and Walter Campbell, Harriet Olcott; (seated, l. to r.) Maud Perry, Charles Barrett, Jessie Messmore, Nannie Olcott, May Leonard, Emma Olcott, Leonard Dakin; (at r.) Marion Olcott, Paul Dakin

Because of her poverty no occasion was more welcome to her than the monthly church suppers across the street. There, as a devoted church worker, Mrs. Woodburn was always on hand to help clear away and wash up. Tarzy, her shadow, stood by with a large tin pan, into which she shovelled leftover edibles. This usually amounted to so much that, with the frequent gifts from her friends and neighbors, she and Tarzy and the twenty-five dependents managed very well to keep body and soul together until the next church supper.

Mrs. Woodburn setting out for a call under her lace-trimmed black parasol was a sight to behold. From her ancient bonnet hung an inevitable long black veil with green chenille dots, under which her hair in great ringlets hung in dignified position. Her cape, made out of black silk carpet rags, looked from the distance like Persian lamb. Her carefully preserved gown was the same one she had worn from time immemorial; no one had ever seen her in any other. Tarzy always tagged along at a proper five paces behind, a cock's feather waving from an old felt hat that was tied securely under her small chin. She wore a grey antique double cape, which only partly concealed an old velveteen shooting coat, and her great shoes that were made of two pieces of heavy cowhide were seventy-five years old. She never appeared without a huge muff, and her hair, done in the style of the 1850's, was held in place by a net made of shoe laces. Mrs. Woodburn explained Tarzy to her friends by saying that the less we investigate her origin the better, for she was found in a hop-yard! And she would add in a whisper with her hand to her mouth, "She has a clouded intellect."

On Sundays Tarzy followed Mrs. Woodburn to church at a respectful distance, carrying her huge Bible. She always sat in the pew behind her mistress, her gloved hands, one in grey and one in brown, resting gently on the back of the pew in front of her. When they went out at night she preceded her mistress, carrying a lantern to light her footsteps.

The minister's wife, Mrs. Swinnerton, who watched Mrs. Woodburn's needs closely, doubtless did the most for her. One day Mrs. Woodburn conceived the idea of giving a dinner party to all those who had been so kind to her. Mrs. Swinnerton went in to help her prepare it and found her, with Tarzy excitedly hovering over, composing a dessert from the innumerable little souvenir boxes of wedding cake she had saved over the past fifty years! These she was blending together with some of Mrs. Cox's excellent homemade elderberry wine into a never-to-be-forgotten pudding. "This I got when Katherine was married," said she, indicating a certain dried-up morsel. (Katherine had been married some thirty years before.) "And this piece came from your own dear mother's wedding!"

Mrs. Woodburn's deep Victorian sense of the proprieties led her to separate her cats, the male from the female. The gentlemen lived in the barn, the ladies on the upper floor in her house. Since neither group was allowed any liberty, her house was sometimes referred to as "the nunnery."

It is said that since Mrs. Woodburn's death, on windy nights cats can be heard crying near her house.

Dickens and "Glorified Lemonade"

IN THE decade of the eighties a Dickens worship pervaded the country and George Dakin was one of its high priests. He read aloud beautifully and spent many hours reading Dickens to his family. From the sleepy attitude of Annie in Plate 118, he might be reading George Meredith, but it is far more likely that, with a slight tremor in his fine, deep voice, he has just finished the death of Little Nell and his wife is feeling it deeply.

Wherever books were found, there were sets of Dickens, Thackeray, and Scott, whose popularity far outweighed that of the current American authors. Leonard Dakin was a boy in London when he first read *Ivanhoe*, in a cheap fine-print, two-column edition of 1868. He loved it so much that his father had the volume rebound for him in Rome in marbled boards and tooled leather, one of the few fancily bound books in the Dakins' library.

All the favorite young people's books of the day were read by the children, some of the little girls finding it hard to wait for Sundays to come around, for from the Sunday School library they drew the Elsie Dinsmore books. Elsie was that pious child who sat one Sunday on the piano stool until she fainted, steadfastly refusing to obey her wicked father's command that she play the piano on the holy day! They enjoyed *The Water Babies*, *Paul and Virginia*, and *Black*

Beauty. They loved *Alice in Wonderland* and all could recite the "Jabberwocky" by heart. It was fun to bewilder an adult caller who had forgotten his *Alice* by looking him in the eye and saying to him quite seriously, "All mimsy were the borogroves, And the mome raths outgrabe." "What strange children!" the adults must have thought. They wept over *Uncle Tom's Cabin*, but the little cousins with a Southern mother (the rebel who had married Egbert Olcott) loved far more that picture of ideal plantation life, *Diddie, Dumps and Tot*. And they all loved *Uncle Remus* of course, but Louisa May Alcott, Frances Hodgson Burnett, and James Fenimore Cooper became favorites. They picnicked so often on Cooper's lake, "Glimmerglass," the scene of *The Pioneers* and *The Deerslayer* where the reeds of Hutter's Island (called the "floating island") were still visible, that they had a proprietary feeling about these particular novels. Great-grandmother Leonard especially enjoyed reading *Swiss Family Robinson* aloud to them. Other favorites were *Gulliver's Travels, Robinson Crusoe, Masterman Ready, Ben Hur,* and *The Scottish Chiefs;* the latter they read over and over. There was a greatly celebrated poem which had appeared originally in *Harper's* in 1857, that revealed with much irony the contrast between the rich and the poor and caused no little controversy. This poem impressed Annie Dakin so deeply that she gave a bound copy of it to her little daughter Floy and bade her commit it to memory. This Floy did and the family took delight in listening to her recite it. The poem told of young Miss Flora McFlimsey of Madison Square who in spite of many, many exhaustive shopping trips to Paris was always

118. September 27, 1887. George Dakin reading aloud under trees: "Aunt Kitty" Wakefield (left), George, Paul, Anna Maria

in a state of utter despair because she had absolutely nothing to wear.

The dime novels of the day, the "yellowbacks," were forbidden the children; but when a number of them were once found hidden in the barn and were given to old Mrs. Culver who helped with the babies, this troubled the children. Why would they not injure Mrs. Culver's morals if they would injure the boys'?

As the girls grew older they sighed over the advice to the lovelorn in Ruth Ashmore's department, "Side Talks with Girls," in the *Ladies' Home Journal*. And they developed a fondness for a certain light and romantic writer who went under the pseudonym of The Duchess. But their reading eventually included most of the New England authors, as well as Ouida, Bulwer, and other well-known British authors. Young Marion, the Dakin children's cousin, who read everything she could lay her hands on, was happy to have discovered George Meredith by herself, and she read all the French, German, and Russian novelists whose translations she could find.

But George Dakin, while a wide reader and collector of all kinds of books, always gave first place to Dickens. He would be the reader when they had a Dickens evening at the church and the reading was illustrated by tableaux by the young people. And he started one of the many Dickens Clubs in Brooklyn, which were so popular at this time.

This was the age when the printed word in the best journals must never offend the most sensitive taste, but there was no danger at "Uplawn," where the favorites were Henry Ward Beecher's religious

119. July 16, 1888. The George Dakins, Anna Maria with her arm around
Paul on the steps of the south porch at "Uplawn"

weekly, the *Independent,* and the *Christian Union,* a news weekly which later became the *Outlook.* They also read *Scribner's* and *Harper's,* and young Harriet Olcott, who adored her older cousin Leonard, sacrificed three dollars from her allowance to give him a subscription to the *Century Magazine* for a Christmas gift.

Grandmother Olcott enjoyed the popular *Fred, Maria and Me,* by Elizabeth Prentiss, a prolific writer of religious novels. When she quoted a line from it one day, a visitor remarked, to her grandchildren's great mirth, "Mrs. Olcott always has an apt quotation from the Bible." But when she became so lost to the world in *Jane Eyre* that she brushed a child aside, she was so conscience-stricken that she vowed never to read another novel. And she never did.

Often the older people sunned themselves on the south porch while George Dakin read to them. Plate 120 shows him in a skull cap at the age of fifty-six, only one year before his death. The south porch was a favorite gathering place, whether for reading or visiting. The sun was warm on the steps and the dense overhanging woodbine gave shade within. The eye of an artist is evident in the composition of Plate 121. The grouping is similar to that in some of Manet's paintings.

The young people of today would smile with incredulity at the next picture (Plate 122). What modern boy would read aloud to the girls as they sat in a hammock and embroidered? But their instincts were not so widely different after all. For often they would tire of the book and run up to Flint's woods to have the gypsies, who

120. July 29, 1890. Enjoying the sun: (on porch railing) George Chamberlain, Anna Maria; (at left) Floy, Leonard; (on steps) Frances Pierson, Ellie Dakin, Jessie (shading Roland's eyes from the sun), Paul, Nannie Olcott, George Dakin wearing a skull cap

camped there every summer, tell their fortunes or read the bumps on their heads. And then perhaps they would go on a little farther to Prospect Hill House for a cooling drink while they watched the sunset over the Mohawk Valley. Gin fizzes were very popular there, as was a special milk punch.

At all the houses lemonade was the common drink between meals and there were always great quantities of it. For a day of special festivities, such as the Fourth of July, Leonard Dakin used to make his famous "glorified lemonade," a luscious fruit-and-liquor punch that was set up in the billiard room in the guest cottage and would last all day. And then there was what came to be known as "Len Dakin's bottled cider." He left the bung loose in a barrel of cider in the fall until it stopped buzzing. Then bunging it up tight he left it in a cold cellar all winter, and when he came north in the spring he bottled it. The young people thought this tasted like champagne!

At dinner, which was served at midday, Cherry Valley roast lamb was the choicest of all meats, but roast beef never appeared on the table at "Uplawn." There were always four or five fresh vegetables from their own garden and Mame's pies were famous. Supper was a light but hot meal. There were no cocktails and no afternoon tea in the eighties, but tea was always served at supper, which itself was often called "tea."

Since their eating and drinking habits were fairly regular and their days filled with exercise, there was little sickness among these young people. But in the spring a general tonic was the custom and a current advertisement for one of the favorites ran as follows:

121. August 30, 1887. Study in sunlight and shade: (on railing) Paul Dakin;
(on bench) Floy, Larry Olmstead; (behind bench) May Vanderlip; (on steps,
upper row) Harvey Loomis, Carrie Clark; (below) Anna Maria, Grace Olmstead, Frank Bainbridge, Daisy Vanderlip

Ayer's Sarsaparilla invariably relieves the evil results of too close application to work and study and gives the freshness of May to the countenance of December.

This was the same Ayer who made the famous Ayer's Cherry Pectoral. Another popular medicine of the time was Dr. Pierce's Golden Medical Discovery which was said to "cure all humors even consumption."

But what was sold in unbelievable quantities was the stuff concocted by the old Medicine Shows which made regular appearances in Cherry Valley. They would stay at the Winne House for a week at a time. There the Medicine Show manager would borrow a wash tub, fill it three-fourths full of water, add his medicinal coloring matter, give it a stir, and proceed unblushingly to fill hundreds of bottles. These they sold for a dollar a bottle between the acts of their hair-raising melodramas. The stuff was called "Katongah," and was guaranteed to cure everything from snake-bite, flea-bite, earache, and sprained ankle to consumption. As the selling agent paced the aisles holding the miracle bottles aloft, excitement reached fever heat while he shouted out its virtues against the blare of his accompanying "slide-trombone," cornet, and bass drum. So many bottles did he sell that it was fortunate for the credulous townspeople that the stuff was harmless.

The cook at the Winne House always managed to fill an extra bottle for herself from the dregs left in the borrowed wash tub. One wonders if those dregs were not left for her on purpose, for she

122. Floy and Eloise Bennett relax in hammock while Harvey Loomis reads to them. Paul swings in hammock at right

proved, in her elation at getting a free bottle, the best kind of advertisement for Katongah. She declared that it cured every ill that she ever had!

Sometimes a pen-and-crayon artist would accompany these Medicine Shows, drawing people's houses to scale and selling the framed pictures for a good price, but offering one free for his own room and board at the Winne House.

123. September 5, 1887. Leonard and Jessie spooning

124. September 5, 1887. Jessie, Leonard's fiancée, poses in a clearing on Tower Hill

Romance

MANY COURTSHIPS were carried on in Cherry Valley during the frequent buggy drives. Leonard Dakin's was no exception, and in these photographs it has reached the point where he and Jessie Messmore are deciding that they will announce their engagement before the summer is over and be married the next winter.

He had fallen in love first of all with the back of her neck, sitting behind her in church. Girls dressed their hair in an upsweep and away from the ears in those days. This made earrings stylish for evening wear and Jessie's ears had been pierced as a child in anticipation of this need. Leonard never knew what the sermon was about when he sat behind those little ears and that lovely neckline.

Not only did they take buggy drives, but they often rode horseback together. One day her horse's girth broke and, since she was riding sidesaddle, she was thrown to the ground. Although her horse carefully stepped over her and she was uninjured, Leonard was so solicitous about her that he placed her in a hammock, covered her up with an afghan, shaded her with a parasol, and then—took her picture. The photograph (Plate 125) turned out to be one of the most artistic in his collection. Again the chiaroscuro makes a pattern that resembles an impressionist painting.

When Jessie's father, Daniel Messmore, was a guest in Cherry

Valley he felt he was amply repaid for walking to the top of Waldron's Grove to get the lovely view from the hills. There through the treetops he could see "Uplawn," its big barn below the house, and the guest cottage across the lawn.

Daniel Messmore had had a colorful history, from the time when, as a lad of nineteen, he had traded barrels of apples with the Indians in northern Wisconsin and brought back from his last trip, besides a goodly sum of money, two baby Wapiti deer. These he decided to take to England and present to Queen Victoria at her coronation. They proved of so much interest to the Earl of Derby, who was in charge of the Royal Zoological Garden, that the Earl entertained young Daniel at his estate for several months and took him as his guest to the coronation, where he made his presentation. For many years thereafter these deer, grown to their full majesty, stood stuffed in Kensington Museum.

Daniel then invested in a ship waterlogged and abandoned off Edenton, North Carolina, and sold at auction by Lloyd's. It was a lucky stroke, for the ship was filled with dry goods destined for the West Indies. Wishing to turn the cargo into cash at once, young Daniel opened a store at Edenton to sell the merchandise off. There he met and fell in love with the beautiful daughter of one of the most distinguished physicians of the South. But her blue-blooded family did not welcome this Yankee merchant as a suitor of Mary Norcom, belle of Edenton. When his goods were sold and he proposed marriage, her brother challenged him to a duel. But he lifted Mary to his horse and galloped away with her, the brother running wildly after

127. September 6, 1888. Paul (left) and Jessie's father, Daniel Messmore
(right), with his granddaughter Mary Campbell and Jessie

would be over her. "It will be full of nice people, ladies and gentle-men, to whom you can apply in any necessity, and who will be as good a protection to you as a traveling companion. . . . You will get your meals in the hotel car."

He instructed her to telegraph him as soon as she had made up her mind to come, to telegraph him again from the station just before leaving, and again from Wilmington or Savannah on the way. He urged her to leave without letting her sister know, or even Mary (Lizzie's daughter who was like a younger sister to Jessie). He asked her not to pack her trunk but to let Mary do that after she was gone. But she needed a confidant, she was so excited, and she knew she could trust Mary.

Mary, thrilled to be part of such a romantic adventure, proved an invaluable aid. She contrived means of keeping her mother away from the house while the two girls together packed the bridal trunk and got it off. The already close bond between them was strengthened as Mary's love and sympathy stiffened Jessie's purpose and made her less fearful that Lizzie would hear her pounding heart. At last with high courage and with bag in hand, she told her sister that she was going to Manhattan to spend the night with a friend, and then she went to see her father.

With no explanation at all she asked him for a large sum of money and her mother's silver tea set. Without a question he opened the safe and gave her what she wanted. When he gently kissed her good-by she believed that he guessed where she was going, but no word was said. On the train she met a kindly old gentleman to whom

128. Mrs. Daniel Messmore with her ninth baby, Jessie
From a daguerreotype

129. Jessie Messmore at the time of
her elopement to Florida
Photographer unknown

130. Leonard's dog and cat welcome the bride at breakfast

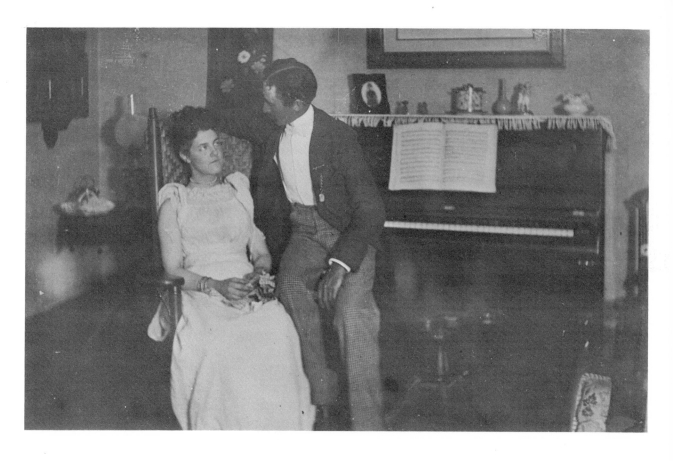

131. Jessie and Leonard dressed for evening at "Racimo," their home in Florida

132. George, Anna Maria, and Floy having lunch by the riverside at "Racimo"

she poured out her whole story; it was a comfort to have someone to talk to.

Leonard met her at Jacksonville as planned and dear old Mrs. Wakefield (always called "Aunt Kitty") took her to her bosom. In her pleasant home they were married on January 26, 1889. Immediately afterward Jessie took great delight and satisfaction in telegraphing her sister: "Married today. Well and happy."

After the honeymoon, spent in the lovely Ponce de Leon Hotel in St. Augustine, Leonard took his bride to "Racimo," their grove in Georgetown. In Plate 130 she wears a corsage at breakfast, and she protects her pretty challis dress from the dog's mouth with a handkerchief. The dog is wearing a bow of ribbon around his neck in honor of his new mistress, and the cat on the piano stool adds a note of domesticity.

The bridegroom's outfit in this next photograph is rather puzzling—checked trousers and a stiff bosom shirt with no vest! The little gold locket in which he carried Jessie's picture for so many years may be seen on the watch chain hanging from his coat pocket.

When Leonard's parents and his sister Floy joined them later that winter, he made many photographs of their life in Florida, of which these few will serve as samples. Since no railway reached Georgetown, all traffic and shipping of fruit was by boat through Palatka on the St. John's River. "Racimo" was a large plantation with some five thousand orange trees, forty laborers, and a big packing house. Jessie Dakin, the young bride, loved the life at the grove, often visiting the packing house and helping to wrap each

133. Floy and her parents under moss-draped live oaks

orange in tissue paper before it was packed in its crate. Willie Babbitt was the faithful overseer, of whose six motherless children Jessie and Floy grew very fond.

Leaving "Racimo" in charge of Willie Babbitt, the Dakins returned to "Uplawn" in Cherry Valley in the summer. Here in 1890 (Plate 137) is Jessie at the age of twenty-four, with her first baby, Roland Norcom. (Only about two yards of the baby's dress got into the picture!) This is another of Leonard's most appealing photographs, with its unusual lighting effects and beauty of composition. Paul's expression is meditative, and one wonders what he is thinking as he stands by the piazza rail looking at this modern Madonna. He had fallen in love with Jessie first and had engaged to drive her alone in a buggy to that eventful supper at Casler's where his brother won the kiss. But Paul had been late for some reason in calling for her, and Leonard drove off with his girl!

With the arrival of this baby, the first of the Dakins' three children, we leave behind that golden decade of peace and serenity— the eighties. Early in the next decade, with the grove at "Racimo" completely wiped out by frost, the Dakins gave up their winter home in Florida. They returned to Cherry Valley, where Leonard became cashier and later president of the bank. From then on he had little time for photography except for an occasional picture of his family.

In Plate 139 he caught Jessie and their children watching old Tompy as she was milking their loved cow, gentle Fawn. It was a daily ritual for the children to sit on the fence in the evening to wait for their supper milk, for they loved to drink it warm.

134. March 29, 1889. St. John's River, Florida. Jessie (top, in white) on
steamer from Palatka to Georgetown

The next photograph shows the three Dakin children when they were older. Of all the pictures Leonard Dakin took, he loved best the one of his little boy Herbert asleep on a garden bench. It is he but for whose wisdom in preserving the plates of these photographs, we never should have had this record of the "Happy Valley."

"Woodbine" no longer stands and "Uplawn" has been sold. No Olcotts or Dakins live in Cherry Valley now, but their children's children still love to return to the village and wander in the old gardens listening for echoes of the past.

135. Floy and a friend midst palmettos on the St. John's River, Florida

136. Willie Babbitt and his children

137. "Uplawn," 1890. The proud grandfather,
George, and Paul Dakin take pleasure
in Jessie and her baby Roland

138. South porch at "Uplawn":
(l. to r.) Mrs. Fox and Mr. Eddy,
who founded Eddy (now
Carlsbad), New Mexico,
Jessie with Roland, Floy

139. Jessie and her three children waiting for their supper. The older boy is Roland Norcom, the younger boy is Herbert Leonard, and the little girl sucking her thumb is the present author

140. Roland, Pauline, and Herbert Dakin in the late nineties

141. Herbert Leonard Dakin at age three, his father's favorite picture
Reproduced from a blueprint by L. Dakin, 1896

BIBLIOGRAPHY and APPENDIX

Selected Bibliography

Allen, Frederick Lewis. *Only Yesterday*. New York: Harper & Bros., 1931.

Beer, Thomas. *The Mauve Decade*. New York: Knopf, 1926.

Branch, Edward Douglas. *The Sentimental Years, 1836-1860*. New York: Appleton-Century, 1934.

Brown, Harriet C. *Grandmother Brown's Hundred Years, 1827-1927*. Boston: Little, Brown & Co., 1929.

Campbell, William W. *The Annals of Tryon County: or, The Border Warfare of New-York During the Revolution*. New York: J. & J. Harper, 1831.

Canby, Henry Seidel. *The Age of Confidence: Life in the Nineties*. New York: Farrar & Rinehart, 1934.

Cherry Valley Gazette, Cherry Valley, N.Y. Old issues in the Cherry Valley Memorial Library.

Cox, Abraham Beekman. *Recollections of "Aunty-Grandma" Cornelia Beekman Schwartz*. Cherry Valley, N.Y.: privately printed, 1932.

Dunbar, Seymour. *A History of Travel in America*. Vols. I and II. Indianapolis: Bobbs-Merrill Co., 1915.

Earle, Alice Morse. *Stage-coach and Tavern Days*. New York: Macmillan, 1900.

Egan, Maurice Francis. *Recollections of a Happy Life*. New York: George H. Doran Co., 1924.

Leaning, Mary S. *Lectures on the One Hundred Twenty-Ninth Anniversary of the Cherry Valley Massacre*. Cherry Valley Chapter of the Daughters of the American Revolution, 1907.

Little, Mrs. William S. *The Story of the Massacre at Cherry Valley*. Paper before the Rochester Historical Society, 1890.

Mumford, Lewis. *The Brown Decades: A Study of the Arts in America, 1865-1895*. New York: Harcourt, Brace & Co., 1931.

Nevins, Allan. *The Emergence of Modern America, 1865-1878*. New York: Macmillan, 1927. Vol. VIII of the series "A History of American Life."

Newhall, Beaumont. *The History of Photography*. New York: The Museum of Modern Art, 1964.

Reed, Amy Louise. "Female Delicacy in the Sixties," in *Century Magazine*, October, 1915.

Sawyer, John. *History of Cherry Valley From 1740 to 1898*. Cherry Valley, N.Y.: privately printed, 1898.

Schlesinger, Arthur H. *Learning How to Behave: A Historical Study of American Etiquette Books*. New York: Macmillan, 1946.

Swinnerton, Henry U. *The Story of Cherry Valley*. Cherry Valley, N.Y.: privately printed, 1908.

Taft, Robert. *Photography and the American Scene: A Social History, 1839-1889*. New York: Macmillan, 1938.

Towle, George M. *American Society*. London: Chapman and Hall, 1870.

Toynbee, Arnold J. *Civilization on Trial*. New York: Oxford University Press, 1948.

Wecter, Dixon. *The Saga of American Society*. New York: Scribner's, 1937.

White, Lydia L. *Success in Society: Manual of Good Manners*. Boston: James H. Earle, 1888.

Woodward, W. R. *The Way Our People Lived*. New York: Dutton & Co., 1944.

Wright, Richardson Little. *Hawkers and Walkers in Early America*. Philadelphia: Lippincott, 1927.

Appendix: A Technical Note on Dakin's Photography

LEONARD DAKIN took up photography at a most critical and challenging point in its history. The gelatine plate, invented by Richard Leach Maddox, had been so greatly improved by others that in 1886 snapshots could regularly be taken. "Instantaneous photography" was all the rage and the boldest experiments in stopping action were made by amateurs. W. F. Carlton, a Rochester camera manufacturer, wrote in 1885:

> Instantaneous photography possesses a fascination peculiar to itself; the amateur feels a particular desire to "take something" and if the "something" be an animate object unconscious of his presence so much the better, and with what a thrill does he see his first "snapshot" develop up, whether a railroad train, a trotting horse, or a man hurrying along the ground whom he has transfixed with one foot on the ground, the other in the air, and his whole figure in an attitude that the original would repudiate, and declare he had never assumed such a position, were not the proof against him.*

Cameras were produced in the 1880's in great variety to satisfy

*W. F. CARLTON, *The Amateur Photographer*, 2d ed., Rochester, 1885, p. 35. (Note that this does not appear in the first edition of 1884.)

259

demands of amateurs. Dakin owned two cameras: a "Premo" for 5 x 7 inch plates, made by the Rochester Optical Company, and a "Champion" sold by E. and H. T. Anthony for 5 x 8 inch plates. Since the "Premo" line of cameras was not put on the market until 1893, the camera Dakin used for his action pictures of the 1880's must have been the "Champion." It was of the type called a view camera, which was intended to be used on a tripod. It had no finder or focusing device: the photographer threw a black cloth over the camera and his head and observed the upside-down image on the ground glass. The lens was a "No. 2 Hémisphèrique Rapide," manufactured by Alphonse Darlot of Paris. This was a good rapid rectilinear, consisting of two symmetrical elements.

There was a slot in the middle of the brass barrel, between the elements, into which could be slipped a metal mask to reduce the aperture of the lens. Four of these "Waterhouse Stops" were neatly stored in a leather case fastened to the lens cap; they were marked 20, 8, 5, 3, indicating the diameter of each aperture in millimeters.

Dakin made his exposures with a drop shutter, which he adapted to work more quickly with rubber bands. The drop shutter was simply a rectangular piece of wood or metal with a hole in its center, which slid vertically in a frame fastened on the front of the lens. Before exposure the shutter was raised so that the solid bottom covered the lens and held in place with a catch. To make a snapshot the catch was released, and the board dropped by gravity, uncovering the lens as the hole flashed by. The exact speed of Dakin's shutter is not known, but Prof. L. H. Laudy of Columbia College tested a similar shutter in 1885 and found by photographing a tuning fork arrangement and counting the number of vibrations recorded that the exact exposure was 1/13 second.* Prof. Laudy then measured the speed of drop shutters fitted with rubber bands to speed up their action; he found that with three rubber bands the exposure measured 1/108 second. He could not make it work any faster.

The minimum shutter speed required to stop action depends on the direction of the action in respect to the axis of the camera. According to Cassell's *Cyclopaedia of Photography* (London, 1912), an exposure of 1/150 second is required to photograph a man running and jumping toward the camera. A side view of this action requires 1/450 second. Dakin was, therefore, just able to stop action with his equipment by limiting his camera position to head-on shots. Since his camera was not fitted with a finder or focusing scale, he chose a fixed point on which to focus—the tennis net or jump rope.

There were many other shutters on the market giving speeds much shorter than 1/100 second; it is surprising that Dakin was content with the primitive drop-shutter-cum-elastic bands.

It is extraordinary that with his limited equipment Dakin was able to photograph his agile friends with such verve and exuberance; one wonders what he would have produced had he used the more advanced equipment then available.

BEAUMONT NEWHALL

*L. H. LAUDY, "Determination of Intervals of Exposure," *Anthony's Phot. Bul.*, Dec. 12, 1885, p. 726.

261